THE CHILDREN'S ILLUSTRATED
ENCYCLOPEDIA
of
HEAVEN

This book is for my father, Puranmal Ganeriwala,
with much love.

THE CHILDREN'S ILLUSTRATED
ENCYCLOPEDIA
of
HEAVEN

ANITA GANERI

ELEMENT
CHILDREN'S BOOKS

SHAFTESBURY, DORSET • BOSTON, MASSACHUSETTS • MELBOURNE, VICTORIA

First published in Great Britain in 1999 by
ELEMENT CHILDREN'S BOOKS,
The Old School House, Bell Street,
Shaftesbury, Dorset SP78BP

Published in the U.S.A. in 1999 by
ELEMENT BOOKS INC.
160 North Washington Street
Boston MA 02114

Published in Australia in 1999 by
ELEMENT BOOKS and distributed by
Penguin Books Australia Limited,
487 Maroondah Highway,
Ringwood, Victoria 3134

Designed and created for ELEMENT BOOKS by MCKELLAR-STOREY

ELEMENT BOOKS LIMITED
Managing Director/Publisher Barry Cunningham
Production Director Susan Sutterby

MCKELLAR-STOREY
Editorial Director Shona McKellar
Art Director Rita Storey
Picture Research Fiona Corbridge

Cover Designed by Dominic Owen
Cover Illustration by Holly Warburton

Reproduction by Renaissance, U.K.
Printed and bound in Italy by Graphicom

British Library Cataloguing in Publication data available
Library of Congress Cataloging in Publication data available

ISBN 1 90261812 2

Publisher's note:
This book uses American English spelling and punctuation.

CONTENTS

INTRODUCTION

ONE of the most difficult questions of all to answer is what happens to us when we die. Is there another life to look forward to? And does the way we live today affect what happens in the hereafter? For many people Heaven helps to make sense of our lives on Earth by giving us comfort and purpose. Indeed, the hope of Heaven is often hope for the future.

OF course, as with all the most difficult questions, there is more than one answer to what happens next. If you ask ten people for their ideas about Heaven, you would probably get ten different answers! Some people treat Heaven as a real place, a wonderful reward for a good life on Earth. To reach it, we must follow specific rules. Others use Heaven as a state of mind, a symbol of what we can achieve by our good behavior. Other people say Heaven begins here on Earth, not when our lives reach an end. By trying to make this world a better place, we can create a Heaven for everyone to share in the here and now.

In this book, you will find out what people from different faiths, cultures and backgrounds believe about Heaven. There are no hard and fast answers. Even within the same religion, people may hold different views. We have also asked many ordinary people to share their personal hopes, fears and feelings. It isn't possible to include everything – there are too many answers for one book! And the book does not try to tell you *what* to think. Rather it tries to *make* you think – about life and death, and the hope of Heaven. Where you will ultimately find it is really up to you!

Anita Ganeri

Take all the pleasures of the spheres,
And multiply each through endless years –
One minute of Heaven is worth them all.

Thomas Moore
Lalla Rookh

HEAVENS ABOVE

WHERE do you think Heaven is? What is it like and how do you get there? Heaven means different things to different people. In some religions, people believe that Heaven is an actual place. As a sort of reward, people who lead good lives on Earth are thought to go to Heaven when they die. Other people have different ideas. A Chinese proverb says, "Heaven and Hell are within the heart." They think that Heaven is a state of mind. For example, it may mean feeling happy or doing someone a good turn. They say that Heaven is inside us all. You just have to look and you'll find it.

BEING WITH GOD

MANY people believe that Heaven is a beautiful place where God lives. When good people die, their souls go to Heaven to be with God for ever. In Heaven, they live in perfect peace and happiness, free from all worries and cares. But Heaven does not have to be an actual place. For many people, worshiping God and having God in their lives is Heaven. Living without God is Hell.

STEPS TO HEAVEN

PEOPLE have tried many ways of reaching Heaven. In Ancient Egypt, the sloping sides of a pyramid were seen as a staircase to the skies. The soul of the dead king buried inside walked up the stairs to join the sky god. This is also the reason why, over the centuries, people have built towering churches and temples for worshiping God. They believed that the higher they built, the closer it brought them to Heaven.

"I think Heaven is a place you go to when you die but only if you've been good. It's a place in the sky where everything is peaceful and you can meet God. If you've been naughty, you go to Hell. That's a fiery, underground place near the center of the Earth where the devil lives."

Thomas Wynne aged 11

PICTURES OF HEAVEN

CLOSE your eyes and think of Heaven. What do you see? You might imagine Heaven as a safe, happy place, like being tucked snugly in bed while a terrible storm rages outside. It might be a place filled with fun and laughter, or with peace and quiet. Or it could be a place full of all your favorite people and things. Some people believe that, in Heaven, they will be reunited with loved ones who have died. Thinking that one day you will see them again helps to stop people feeling so sad and alone.

HEAVEN ON EARTH

OF course, you don't have to be dead to be in Heaven. You can always create your own Heaven on Earth. It's up to you what it is like. Perhaps it is listening to your favorite music or seeing your team win at football. Or it might be going out for a pizza or taking your dog for a walk. It might be trying to be a better, kinder sort of person, or having a best friend. It's really up you!

THE OTHER PLACE

WHAT happens if you don't make it to Heaven? Watch out, you might end up in Hell instead! Hell was often shown as a dreadful place underground where bad people were sent to be punished, far away from God's love and care. This frightened people into obeying the rules of their religion. Other people thought Hell showed how unhappy people's lives would be without God. But other things can be hellish, too, such as wars, famines and the threat from terrible diseases, such as cancer or AIDS. On an everyday level, Hell could be as simple as having to go to school even though you hated it. What do you think?

In Islamic belief, Heaven, or Paradise, is like a beautiful, refreshing garden. It is a place of perfect peace and happiness.

Pictures *of* Heaven

FOR thousands of years, people have tried to imagine what they think Heaven will be like. Of course, no one really knows for sure. For many people, Heaven is a real place. It is often located in the sky among the clouds and stars, in the highest part of the universe. There are many descriptions of Heaven as a beautiful garden, or Paradise, or a fabulous city, filled with dazzling light. It is a peaceful place where there is no pain or suffering, only joy, happiness and all your heart's desires. For some people Heaven can be found on Earth, among snow-capped mountains, on faraway islands or down in the depths of the sea. Other people believe in Heaven as a state of mind, a way of living and behaving.

CHRISTIAN HEAVEN

For Christians, Heaven is where God is. When they die, they hope their souls will go to Heaven to begin a new life with God. Heaven is sometimes pictured as an actual place, high up in the sky, a beautiful place of light and joy where God has his kingdom. Here, the souls of people who have worshiped God on Earth live in perfect peace with the saints and angels. But Heaven can also be found on Earth. It means having God helping you through life, and living as God wants you to. The joy this brings can be Heaven.

VISION OF HEAVEN

In the Book of Revelation in the Bible, St. John paints this vivid picture of Heaven: "I looked and saw a door to Heaven, and a voice, like a trumpet, said to me, 'Come'. There I saw God sitting on an emerald throne, surrounded by a rainbow. To the left and right were 24 smaller thrones where 24 wise men sat, wearing shining white robes and golden crowns. Behind them stood the hosts of angels. And in front of the throne was a crystal sea. At each corner were four strange beasts, each with six wings and many eyes. Day and night, they sang, 'Holy, holy, holy, Lord God Almighty, who was, and is, and is to come.'"

THE SON OF GOD

CHRISTIANS follow the teachings of Jesus Christ, a man who lived about 2,000 years ago. They believe that Jesus was the son of God. When he was only 33 years old, Jesus was put to death for his beliefs. But Christians think that he came back to life again. This is called the Resurrection. Then Jesus went up to Heaven to join God, his father. Christians believe that the Resurrection shows that people who follow Jesus need not be afraid of death. They, too, will find new life in Heaven.

Jesus also taught that people could create Heaven for themselves by showing love and kindness to other people, and treating them as they would want other people to treat them.

THERE

by Mary Coleridge

There, in that other world, what waits for me?
What shall I find after that other birth?
No stormy, tossing, foaming, smiling sea,
But a new Earth.

No sun to mark the changing of the days,
No slow, soft falling of the alternate night,
No moon, no star, no light upon my ways,
Only the Light.

No grey cathedral, wide and wondrous fair,
That I may tread where all my fathers trod.
Nay, nay, my soul, no house of God is there,
But only God.

THE LORD'S PRAYER

This is a prayer which Jesus taught to his friends and followers.

Our Father who is in Heaven
Hallowed be your name,
Your kingdom come,
Your will be done,
On Earth as it is in Heaven.
Give us today our daily bread.
Forgive us our wrong-doings
As we forgive those who have
wronged us.
Lead us not into temptation
But deliver us
from evil.

JEWISH HEAVEN

TEACHINGS about Heaven and life after death are not very important in Judaism. Jews are much more concerned with how we live our lives on Earth and what happens to us in the here and now. Even so, many Jewish people also believe that Heaven is God's home where the souls of good people go to be with God.

HEAVEN HERE AND NOW

MANY Jews believe that there is life after death and that your soul lives on when your body dies. This idea helps to bring comfort and support, particularly when a loved one dies. They believe that your soul is very precious and needs to return to where it came from. This place may be called Heaven. But they are also concerned with this world, and in making it a better place. They believe it is our duty to repair the damage we have done to the world.

This Jewish rabbi, or teacher, is reading from the Torah, the Jews' holy book. He uses a silver pointer called a yad to point to the words because the book is too precious to touch. He is wearing a prayer robe over his shoulders. For Jews and many other people, prayer is a very important way of talking to God in Heaven.

"When you die, Heaven is where you go in the sky. Your body dissolves in the ground and your spirit goes up to Heaven. There you meet other people who have died. If you don't go to Heaven you just stay in the ground."

Eden Silver-Myer
aged 7

14

THE RABBI AND THE TWO DOORS

THERE was once a rabbi who wanted to see Heaven and Hell for himself. God answered his prayers.

The rabbi found himself in front of a door with no name. The door opened and he peeked inside. In the room beyond, a table was laid for a sumptuous feast with a huge dish of delicious food which made his mouth water. People sat around the table with spoons in their hands but instead of eating, they were crying out in hunger, and cursing God. They tried to eat but they could not. Their spoons had such long handles that they could not reach their mouths with the food. The rabbi realised he was seeing Hell. Quickly, he shut the door.

He closed his eyes and begged God to take him away from this terrible place. But, to his horror, when he opened them again, he saw the same door with no name. Again, the door opened and he peeked inside, into the same room. There was the table and the steaming bowl, and the people with their long spoons. But this time, the shrieks and cries were gone, and the curses had turned to blessings. This time, people were using their long spoons to feed each other! The rabbi realized this was Heaven.

And so the rabbi saw both Heaven and Hell, and the very thin line between them.

A Jewish prayer
O Thou who art at home
Deep in my heart
Enable me to join you
Deep in my heart.
The Talmud

HEAVEN IN ISLAM

Where better to find Heaven than in a beautiful garden, filled with fragrant flowers and gushing fountains? This is how Muslims think of Paradise.

FOR **Muslims, Heaven or Paradise, is a place where people who have followed Allah (God) faithfully on Earth will live forever, close to Allah, in perfect peace and joy. Not everyone goes to Heaven, though. One day in the future, on the Day of Judgement, Allah will judge them according to how well or wickedly they have lived. (See p.32). The reward for a good life is Paradise. But the punishment for a sinful life is to suffer in Hell. Your fate is up to you!**

GOD'S MESSENGER

ALLAH chose a man called Muhammad as his prophet, to carry his message to the world. Muhammad was born in 570 CE. One day, as he was meditating on Mount Hira, Allah sent down the angel Jibril to give him the words of the Qur'an. Muslims believe that these are Allah's very own words, sent down from Heaven. Muhammad learned the words and his friends wrote them down. Muhammad spent the rest of his life teaching people how to follow the word of Allah.

DESERT GARDEN

IN the Qur'an, the Muslim holy book, Paradise is described as a beautiful garden, to which an angel leads you through a gate made of emeralds. Inside, even the soil smells sweet like perfume and the rocks and pebbles are made of jewels and gold. Birds sing and flowers bloom. There is one tree so large you could ride beneath its shade for a whole year and not come to the other side. A refreshing breeze blows, which is never too hot or too cold. It is said that one needle's-eye of Heaven's beauty would cure all the ills of this world. To the people of Arabia – the hot, dry desert country where Islam began about 1400 years ago – the idea of a cool, shady garden must have seemed like Paradise indeed. Later Muslim rulers often planted beautiful gardens around their palaces, to give them a taste of Paradise.

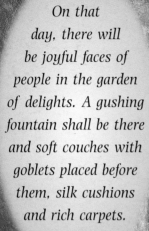

> On that day, there will be joyful faces of people in the garden of delights. A gushing fountain shall be there and soft couches with goblets placed before them, silk cushions and rich carpets.
>
> **The Qur'an, surah 37:47**

THIS is the story of how the Prophet Muhammad rode up into Paradise where Allah taught him how Muslims should pray five times a day. Each year, Muslims remember his journey by praying through the night.

One night, the Prophet Muhammad lay asleep near the Sacred Mosque in Makkah (Mecca). He was woken by the angel, Jibril (also called Gabriel), who took him on an incredible journey. Riding on the back of a white, winged beast, Muhammad sped through the skies to Jerusalem. There he met three of the prophets who had come before him – Ibrahim, Musa, and Isa – and led them in prayer.

Then the angel led Muhammad up a ladder of light, up through the seven Heavens, and into Allah's glorious presence. There Allah told him that Muslims should pray 50 times a day. On his way back to Earth, Muhammad met Musa who asked him what Allah had said. When he heard, he told Muhammad:

"People are too lazy to say so many prayers. Go back and ask your Lord for less."

So Muhammad returned to Allah and ten prayers were taken off. Several times more Muhammad met Musa and the same thing happened, until there were only five prayers left. Muhammad was ashamed to ask for less. Instead he said:

"Whoever says his or her prayers faithfully, five times a day, will have the reward for 50." Then, before daybreak, Muhammad rode away once more, all the way back to Makkah.

> "I think Heaven is a place of peace. I think Heaven is made out of gold. I think the sun will always be shining in Heaven and that the light will be the brightest and loveliest light ever seen."
>
> **Nazir Khalifa aged 11**

HINDU HEAVENS

HINDUS believe that when you die your soul is born again in a different body. This is called reincarnation. It happens time and time again until you can break out of the cycle of dying and being reborn. This breaking free is called *moksha*. People can only reach moksha by replacing their ignorance with wisdom. For some Hindus, moksha is like reaching Heaven. But Hindus also believe in various Heavens as places where the gods and goddesses live, and where your soul rests in between its lives on Earth. These are like stopping off points on your soul's long journey.

REACHING THE SEA

THE cycle of dying and being born again in which your soul is trapped is called *samsara*. Hindus call a person's soul *atman*. Reaching moksha means breaking free from samsara once and for all. It also means that your atman returns to Brahman, the great soul or spirit which some Hindus call God. Hindus describe this as being like a river flowing into the sea so that their waters mix and mingle into one.

DOING YOUR DUTY

THE power which keeps the cycle of life turning is called *karma*. This means your actions, good or bad, and their effects, good or bad. Good karma in this life will mean a good birth next time. Bad karma means your next life will be hard. Hindus believe that there are four main ways, or paths, to moksha. These are knowledge, meditation, loving worship, and duty. People often follow different paths at different times of their lives.

HOMES OF THE GODS

HINDUS divide the world into three parts – the Earth, the sky, and the different levels of Heaven. Depending on your karma, your soul moves up or down through these levels. The higher you go, the better! Each of the important Hindu gods also has a heavenly home, hidden in the clouds around Mount Meru, a mythical mountain in the Himalayas, said to mark the very center of the Universe.

The River Ganges runs through northern India. It is the Hindus' holiest river. Bathing in its water is said to wash away your sins and bring you closer to moksha.

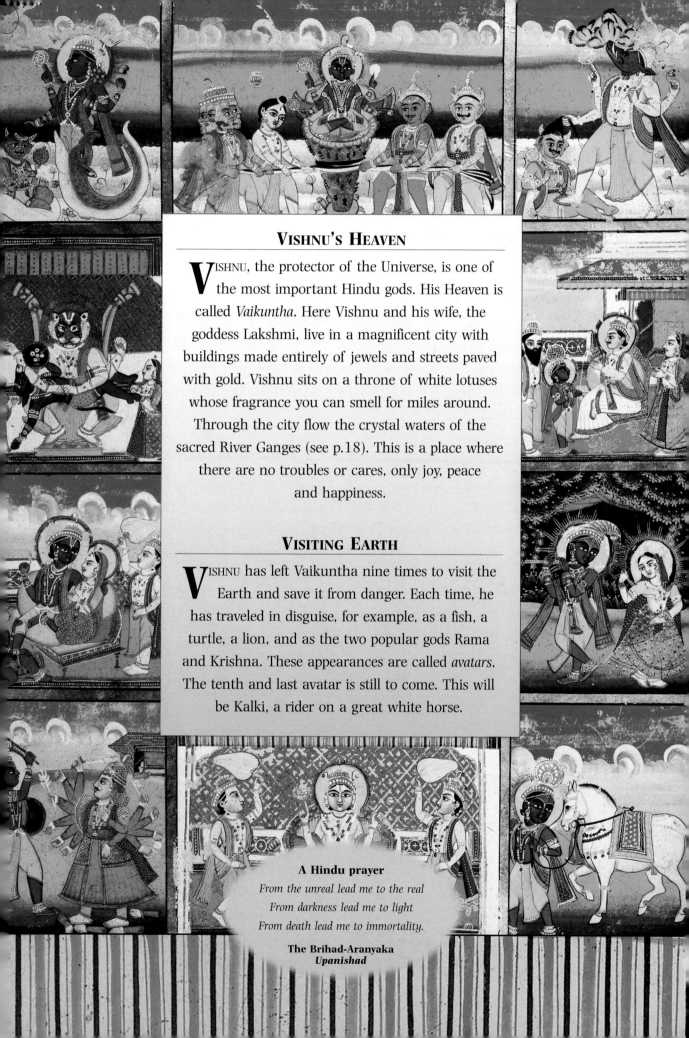

VISHNU'S HEAVEN

VISHNU, the protector of the Universe, is one of the most important Hindu gods. His Heaven is called *Vaikuntha*. Here Vishnu and his wife, the goddess Lakshmi, live in a magnificent city with buildings made entirely of jewels and streets paved with gold. Vishnu sits on a throne of white lotuses whose fragrance you can smell for miles around. Through the city flow the crystal waters of the sacred River Ganges (see p.18). This is a place where there are no troubles or cares, only joy, peace and happiness.

VISITING EARTH

VISHNU has left Vaikuntha nine times to visit the Earth and save it from danger. Each time, he has traveled in disguise, for example, as a fish, a turtle, a lion, and as the two popular gods Rama and Krishna. These appearances are called *avatars*. The tenth and last avatar is still to come. This will be Kalki, a rider on a great white horse.

A Hindu prayer
From the unreal lead me to the real
From darkness lead me to light
From death lead me to immortality.

The Brihad-Aranyaka
Upanishad

BUDDHIST HEAVENS

"When
I have climbed
up a high
mountain
I lie there and look at
the sky and feel close
to Heaven."

**Novice Buddhist
nun
aged 14**

LIKE Hindus, Buddhists believe in reincarnation. But they do not think that people have souls. Instead, each person is made up of five parts – body, feelings, perception, will, and consciousness. These can be taken apart and put back together again in many different ways. This and karma (see p.18) determine what your next life will be like. You are born and die many times until you finally gain enlightenment. This means seeing the truth about how things really are. Then you can reach Nirvana, a state of perfect peace and happiness which some Buddhists think of as being like Heaven.

PERFECT PEACE

BUDDHISTS believe that the cycle of life goes round and round like a wheel, until you can break free and reach Nirvana. They say that Nirvana is like a candle suddenly being blown out. It is the end of everything that is not perfect. This is another description of Nirvana from a Buddhist holy book:

"There is an island, an island which you cannot go beyond. It is a place of nothingness, a place of no possessions and no attachments. It is the total end of death and decay, and this is why I call it Nirvana, the extinguished, the cool."

A monk meditating in the lotus position. Meditation helps create a calm, peaceful mind so that you can gain true insight and enlightenment. The Buddha himself achieved enlightenment while meditating under a tree.

THE PATH TO HEAVEN

To reach Nirvana, Buddhists follow the teachings of the Buddha, a man who lived in India some 2,500 years ago. (Buddha means "the enlightened one".) The Buddha realized that people suffered and were unhappy because they always wanted more. They were never content with what they had.
He taught a way of living so that people could leave unhappiness behind and reach Nirvana. His teaching was like a path leading people to Heaven.

Buddhist Prayer

Didn't I tell you it was there?
You could have found it without trouble, after all.
The south wind is warm.
The sun shines peacefully;
The birds warble their glad songs.
Spring blossoms in the treetops.

Louis Nordstrom (trans.)
Namu Dai Bosa

LEVELS OF HEAVEN

Some Buddhists also believe in different Heavens where past and future Buddhas live, and where you rest in between your births on Earth. One of the most important is Tushita Heaven where Maitreya, the Buddha to come, lives. He will come to Earth in about 30,000 years' time to remind people of the right way to live.

THE PURE LAND

One of the most beautiful Heavens is the Pure Land where a Buddha called Amitabha lives. Buddhists who follow Amitabha hope to be reborn in the Pure Land on their way to Nirvana. They believe that reciting or chanting Amitabha's name will help them on their journey. The Pure Land is described as a peaceful garden, with sweet-smelling rivers and lakes filled with giant lotus flowers, some several miles (kilometers) around. Gold and jewels grow on the trees which flourish along the river banks. All around, birds chirp and sing and bells ring out. There is no pain, sickness or suffering. A heavenly place indeed!

JAIN AND SIKH HEAVENS

This Jain painting of the Universe shows part of the middle world, between Heaven and Hell. The circle in the center stands for Mount Meru, a magical mountain said to be at the very center of the world. Mount Muru is also important for Hindus and Buddhists.

THE Jain religion began in India in the sixth century BCE and most of its followers still live there today. Jains do not believe in a god but worship 24 teachers called *tirthankaras* and use them as guides in their daily lives.

The Sikh religion was started in India about 500 years ago by a holy man, called Guru Nanak. He taught a new way of thinking which stressed tolerance and equality of all. Many Sikhs still live in India but there are also large communities in Britain and the U.S.A.

RESPECT FOR LIFE

THE supreme teacher of the Jain religion is called Mahavira, the last and greatest of the tirthankaras. He came down from Heaven to save the world. Jains believe in karma and rebirth. Every living thing, however small, has a soul which lives on after death. The way to reach moksha (see p.18) is to follow the Three Jewels of "right faith, right conduct, and right knowledge." You should also care for all living things (see p.34) and not harm them.

LEVELS OF LIGHT

JAINS picture the Universe in three parts. These are the underworld, or Hell, the Earth, where humans live, and a series of Heavens where the pure souls live. These get brighter and brighter the higher you go. People who reach moksha travel to an even higher realm, at the very top of the world, beyond the highest Heavens. Here they exist in perfect peace, joy, and knowledge.

FILLED WITH GOD

SIKHS also believe in reincarnation. They think that a person's soul comes from God and will one day return to God. This depends on karma but also on God's love and grace. If you love God and help other people, God will set you free from the cycle of birth and death. Then your soul will be with God forever, in utter bliss. This is *mukti*, or salvation.

THE STORY OF THE WEALTHY BANKER

L ONG ago, there lived a rich banker, Duni Chand. He had more money than most people dream of. But he was also very greedy and miserly. One day, Guru Nanak, the first Sikh Guru, came to town and Duni Chand invited him to a special feast. No expense was spared. There were dishes and dishes of delicious food. Then Duni Chand turned to Guru Nanak.

"As you can see," he said, boastfully, "I am a wealthy man. If I can do anything for you, please ask."

Guru Nanak thought for a moment. He looked at all the luxury, then pulled a plain wooden box out of his pocket. From it, he took a fine silver needle.

"You can look after this for me," he told Duni Chand. "And return it to me in Heaven."

Duni Chand almost burst with pride. How important he felt! But when he showed the needle to his wife, she burst out laughing.

"And how are you going to take it with you?" she chortled.

Duni Chand felt rather confused. He ran after Guru Nanak.

"Oh honored Guru," he called. "Please tell me one thing before you go. How can I take this needle with me when I die?"

The Guru looked at Duni Chand kindly and said,

"My friend, if you can't take a tiny needle with you, how will you take all your wealth and riches? In Heaven, your good deeds will be all that matter."

Duni Chand felt ashamed. What a fool he had been. What was the point of keeping all this wealth to himself – he could not take it with him. From that day on, he used his wealth to help the poor. And when he died, he had plenty of good deeds to take to Heaven with him.

"When I say my prayers, I also light an incense stick. I hope that its sweet smell will float up and reach God in Heaven, in the same way that my prayers will."

Navpreet aged 9

A Sikh prayer
Know the real reason why you are here. Collect up your treasure under the Guru's guidance. Make your mind into God's home. If God is with you always, you will not be reborn.

CHINESE HEAVENS

IN China, there were many ideas about Heaven, all mixed up together. It was sometimes pictured among the stars or in some far-distant part of the Earth. Later, it was named T'ien. It was seen as a heavenly court, ruled over by the Jade Emperor. His courtiers were the souls of nobles and other important people turned into gods when they died. The souls of ordinary people went down into the earth, to make the fields more fertile!

*Heaven means
to be one with God.
He who offends against Heaven
has none to whom he can pray.*

Confucius
Analects

SONS OF HEAVEN

HEAVEN watched over life on Earth and kept the Earth in order. The will of Heaven was very important, especially to the Chinese emperors. They called themselves the Sons of Heaven, claiming that Heaven had given them permission to rule. This was called the Mandate of Heaven. The emperor was expected to rule wisely and well. If he did not, the people would rise against him and Heaven would take its mandate away.

HARMONY WITH HEAVEN

THE philosopher, Confucius, lived in the sixth century BCE. Although he taught about Heaven, he was more concerned with how people lived life on Earth. When asked about death, he replied, "If we do not yet know about life, how can we know about death?" In other words, he had enough trouble trying to understand this world, let alone any others! He believed that if people lived good lives, in peace and harmony with their family, their friends and the world, then harmony with Heaven would be bound to follow.

THE WAY TO HEAVEN

ANOTHER philosopher, Lao-tzu, taught that the path to Heaven is called the *Tao*. This is an invisible power or force behind everything. You should try to live in harmony with the Tao, by leading a good life. Then you could set your soul free and become an immortal.

At Chinese funerals, there are many rituals to help your soul rise up to Heaven. Priests walk in front of the funeral procession, carrying a paper crane. The crane represents a messenger from Heaven. It is then burnt, carrying your soul up to Heaven with the flames.

In Chinese beliefs, everything is either *yin* or *yang*, the two great equal but opposite forces of nature. Keeping the two balanced is very important. Yin stands for the Earth, darkness, women and quietness. Yang stands for Heaven, light, men and noise. The curve which divides them shows the constantly changing relationship between the two.

RICE FROM HEAVEN

RICE is a vital food of China, eaten every day. No wonder legend says that it comes from Heaven. After a great flood devastated the Earth, there was very little to eat. From their Heaven on an island far out to sea, the gods decided to help. They sent six animals – a cow and a horse to plough the fields; a sheep for milk; a cock to wake people in the mornings; a guard dog; and a pig which had no work but could always be eaten in an emergency! When the gods asked for a volunteer to carry the rice, only the dog came forward. They dipped him in the heavenly pond, then rolled him in rice grains until they covered his whole body. Then he jumped into the sea. But the water washed the rice away, all except a very few grains clinging to his tail. It was just enough to plant a small field, the first rice field in China.

The yin and yang symbol

Follow the Way of Heaven,
And you will succeed
Without trying.
You will know the answer,
Without asking the question.
All you need will come to you,
Without having to ask for it.
The Way of Heaven is like a vast net.
Though its meshes are wide, it catches
everything.

Lao-Tzu
Tao Te Chi

JAPANESE HEAVENS

The entrance into a Shinto shrine is marked by a wooden gateway called a torii.

IN Shinto, the ancient religion of Japan, Heaven was called Ame. This was the home of the gods where the souls of good or noble people went after death. It was a faraway place high above the Earth, with flowers, trees, and streams, and a heavenly river running through it. It was believed to look very like Japan.

WAY OF THE GODS

FOLLOWERS of Shinto believe in gods or spirits, called *kami*, which live in humans, animals, plants, mountains, trees, the moon, the sea, and all other natural features. The most important is Amaterasu-o-Mikami, the sun goddess. The kami are divided into gods of Heaven and gods of Earth. It is said that the kami were once able to cross to and fro, between the two, over a bridge. But one night when they were sleeping, the bridge collapsed.

FACING DEATH

ZEN is a type of Buddhism followed in Japan. It teaches that death is just another part of life, like the next step on a long path. We should try to accept it without fear. A story is told of a Zen master. As he lay dying, his disciples remembered how much he liked a particular cake. They searched high and low to buy some. The man smiled and began to eat it. As he grew weaker, one disciple asked him if he had any final words for them. "Yes," he replied. "This cake is delicious!" Then he passed away. He lived in the present, right up to his death.

> *"My daily life is dedicated to serving the kami with a true heart. The kami are our ancestors and we must pray to them with respect and sincerity. This is the way to Heaven."*
>
> **A Shinto priest**

BAHA'I HEAVEN

THE Baha'i faith was begun in Persia (modern-day Iran) in the nineteenth century by a man called Baha'u'llah. He is believed to have been a prophet, sent to lead the world into a new age. To bring this about, Baha'is believe that all the different religions should work together to create a world of peace, justice, and equality, and to end prejudice and intolerance.

> "When you die, your body will be buried, but your soul will go up to Heaven. It's like a bird in a cage. Your soul is the bird and your body is the cage. When you die, your soul is set free to rise up to Heaven and progress towards God."
>
> **Tami Hammond-Collins aged 9**

HEAD START IN HEAVEN

BAHA'IS believe that Heaven is the next world, where your soul or spirit goes for ever when you die. It is described as a garden of happiness, or a heavenly river, or like stepping into a sea of light. But it is really where God is, and God is everywhere. Baha'is do not believe in reincarnation. But, to make good progress in the next world, you must lead a good life in this. If you are a good person, your soul will start off closer to God. In other words, you get a head start in Heaven! If you are a bad person, your soul will start off further away from God.

THE KIND GARDENER

WHEN someone dies, Baha'is try not to be too sad. Death is the start of a new life in Heaven where you will be well looked after. Abdu'l-Baha, Baha'u'llah's son, told people to think of God as a kind gardener who takes a shrub from a dry, rocky place and plants it in rich soil where it can flourish and grow. The shrub is like your soul. Saying prayers for the people's souls is very important. It helps them to make progress in Heaven.

NEW HEAVENS

IF you ask people for their pictures of Heaven, almost everyone will tell you something different. New and alternative ideas are being formed all the time. Here are just a few of them, ranging from an everlasting game of cricket to a fish's eye view of eternal heavenly bliss!

OUT OF BABYLON

RASTAFARIANISM began in Jamaica in the 1930s. Its beliefs are based on the Christian Bible, mixed with African traditions. Rastafarians praise God, whom they call Jah. They also worship Emperor Haile Selassie of Ethiopia, Africa, as their messiah and leader. For them, Ethiopia is a type of Heaven, their "promised land." One day, they believe, they will return to Ethiopia from exile in the countries where they were taken as slaves. They call these places of exile "Babylon."

REGGAE MUSIC

WITH its strong beat and often biblical themes, reggae music is a crucial part of Rastafarian culture. This song is by Bob Marley, one of the most famous reggae singers of all.

FOREVER LOVING JAH

by Bob Marley

We'll be forever loving Jah
We'll be forever loving Jah

Some they say see them walking up the street
They say we are going wrong to all the people
*   we meet*
But we won't worry, we don't shed no tears
We found a way to cast away the fears
Forever yeah!

We'll be forever loving Jah
We'll be forever
We'll be forever loving Jah
Forever yes and forever
We'll be forever loving Jah, there'll be no end.

RASTAFARIANS believe that if they worship Jah, they will live for ever. Only wicked people die. Even if a good Rastafarian dies of old age, he is not really dead. The atoms of his body are used again in new-born babies. Here is another explanation:

A NEW AGE

A wide range of ideas makes up New Age beliefs. Many New Age people have looked forward to the Millennium in the year 2000. This would be an exciting time and there have been many predictions made about what might happen. Some people have thought that there would be a great battle between the forces of good and evil, which might be followed by peace. Others have thought that we have been moving into a new time, called the Age of Aquarius, when peace, love, and harmony would rule our lives, rather than greed and conflict. Could this be a picture of Heaven?

HEAVEN ON EARTH

IN the 1970s, a scientist, James Lovelock, put forward the idea that the Earth is a gigantic living, growing being. This idea is known as the Gaia Theory, after the Ancient Greek goddess of the Earth. He believed that our fate and the Earth's fate are closely linked. Unless we treat the Earth well and work in harmony with nature, both the Earth and its people will suffer. Already people are upsetting the balance – factories and cars pour pollution into the air, forests are cut down, land is over farmed. It is vital that we must halt the damage before it is too late. Then we'd have Heaven on Earth.

A GAME OF CRICKET

"Life is like a game of cricket. As long as the player makes the right stroke that each ball merits, he can play on and on for centuries. The only way he can be bowled out is when he plays a wrong stroke. The same is true for a Rastafarian. If he finds the right spiritual way of dealing with life, he will live forever."

Ras Hu-I

From HEAVEN
by Rupert Brooke

*And in that heaven of all their wish
There shall be no more land, say fish*

Living *and* Dying

WHEN someone dies it can be a sad and frightening time. But death is also an important experience which many people find gives extra meaning to life. Because of this, people have many different ideas about what happens when you die.

SOME people believe that a part of you lives on after your body dies. This is called your soul. It is like an invisible spark or spirit deep inside you which does not get old and die. When your body dies, your soul travels on to the next part of its journey. It may go straight to Heaven or to Hell. Or it might rest for a while before it begins a new life on Earth, in another body. To wish the soul a safe journey to the next world, many people hold special ceremonies when a person dies. These are also a chance for people to say goodbye to a loved one and to share not only their sadness but their happy memories.

JUDGEMENT DAY

In some beliefs, Heaven is seen as a place where the souls of people who have lived good lives on Earth go as a reward. Here they live with God for ever, in perfect peace and happiness. But watch out! The souls of people who have been wicked and sinful on Earth are punished by being sent to Hell, to suffer far away from God's love.

GOOD DEEDS, BAD DEEDS

MUSLIMS say that two angels stay with you through your life, writing down your deeds, good and bad. When you die, these deeds go with you. On the Last Day, Allah will bring the dead back to life. Then your book of deeds will be opened and Allah will judge what you deserve. If your good deeds outweigh your bad, an angel will lead you to Paradise. But if your bad deeds are heavier, you will plummet down into Hell. Muslims believe that Allah is a very fair and merciful judge. If you are truly sorry, your bad deeds will be wiped out. Only Allah knows when the Last Day will be.

This picture of the Last Judgement was painted more than 600 years ago. It showed people the fate awaiting them if they misbehaved!

We shall set up just scales on the Day of Resurrection, so that no man shall in the least be wronged. Actions as small as a grain of mustard seed shall be weighed out.

The Qur'an, surah 21:49

32

SHEEP AND GOATS

SOME Christians also believe in a day of judgement, when God will call people to account. According to how you behave on Earth, your soul may be sent to Heaven or to Hell. Jesus used a story to explain this. On the day of judgement, good people will be separated from bad, just as a shepherd divides his sheep from his goats. The sheep are good people who always help others. The goats are people who are greedy and proud. Which seems very unfair on goats! Paintings of the Last Judgement were often put up in churches to warn people to be on their best behavior.

JEWISH BELIEFS

"GOD will take you one by one to him and tell you what your life was really about. Then you will understand the good you did and the bad, and this will be your Heaven and Hell. But after true knowledge comes forgiveness." This is one of many Jewish viewpoints about what happens when you die. Other Jews believe in a day of judgement, as described in the Hebrew Bible. On that day, "Many of them that sleep in the dust of the earth shall awake, some to everlasting life and some to everlasting shame." Other Jews think that doing a good deed is its own reward.

LORD OF THE DANCE

I danced on a Friday
When the sky turned
black;
It's hard to dance
With the devil on your
back.
They buried my body
And they thought I'd
gone
But I am the dance
and I still go on.

Sydney Carter

BEING REBORN

HINDUS, Sikhs and Jains believe that, when you die, your soul is reborn in another body. Whether your next life is a good or a bad one depends on your karma. This means how well or badly you live your present life. Buddhists also believe in reincarnation but not in a soul (see p.20). The aim of life is to escape from the endless round of being born again and again, and to reach God or a state of perfect peace. This is like being in Heaven. But Heaven is also a place where your soul rests in between rebirths.

CHANGING CLOTHES

IN the Hindu holy book, the *Bhagavad Gita*, the god Krishna says that being reborn in a new body is like changing your clothes:
"When a person's clothes wear out, he leaves them behind
And puts on new and different ones.
And so the soul leaves a worn-out body
And puts on a new and different one."

HUMAN OR ANIMAL?

How would you like to be reborn? As a human, a plant, or an animal? A Sikh hymn gives over eight million forms of rebirth, from worms, to birds, to humans. Being born as a human is best because it takes you closer to salvation. As punishment, you might be reborn as an animal. But all living things should be respected because they all have souls. This is why many Hindus, Buddhists and Sikhs are vegetarians. Jains are even stricter. Some wear masks over their noses and mouths to avoid breathing in tiny insects. This prayer sums up their beliefs:

"I ask pardon of all living creatures;
May all of them pardon me.
May I have a friendly relationship with all beings,
And unfriendly with none."

This Buddhist painting shows Yama, god of death, holding up the wheel of life. It shows the cycle of birth, death and rebirth. Around the outside are the stages of a person's life. Inside are different ways in which you could be reborn.

"Treat all people as if they were already your friend, because in a past life they probably have been!"

The Dalai Lama, leader of the Tibetan Buddhists

THE BUDDHA'S PAST LIVES

THE stories of the Buddha's past lives are told in a collection of tales called the *Jatakas*. In this story, the Buddha is born as a prince famous for his generosity, an important Buddhist value.

There was once a prince called Vessantara, who was handsome, brave, and generous. In fact, he was so very generous that he gave away everything he owned. First, the prince was tricked into giving away his great white elephant, Snow Mountain. It was the most precious possession in the kingdom, for it had the power to make the rain fall. When they heard this, some of the people were angry and bitterly complained to the king. They thought Vessantara should have acted more wisely. Vessantara was banished from the kingdom. But before he left, he gave all his money and belongings to charity. Then he went to live in the forest, with his wife and children.

One day, an old Brahmin (priest) came walking past, worn out by years of hard work. His wife had sent him to find some help. So Vessantara gave the Brahmin his own two children, to work for him as servants. Not long afterwards, another man, a beggar, visited Vessantara's hut. He asked Vessantara to give him his wife. Without hesitating, the prince agreed. But the beggar was the god Indra in disguise. He was so impressed by Vessantara's generosity that he reunited him with his wife and children, and led him back home to live happily ever after.

> *"My dad says that when you die, you come back as an insect. I think it would be nice to be my cat. All she does is eat and sleep all day."*
>
> **Anjali**
> **aged 11**

LIVING FOR EVER

How long is time? It seems to vary. We can measure time with clocks and watches but we know that five minutes doesn't always feel the same. When you are waiting to go to a birthday party, five minutes can seem a very long time. But when you're having fun or are wrapped up in what you are doing, time goes by very quickly. On the other hand, a boring lesson in your least favorite subject can seem to last for a week. Now try to imagine a place where time lasts for ever, a place where time doesn't matter any more. . .

HEAVENLY TIME

. . . a place just like Heaven! Some religions believe that, in Heaven, time stands still. In Heaven, your soul lives for ever, for all eternity. You are never in a hurry; you never grow old. This is one of the things that makes Heaven different from Earth. In some religions, the idea of living for ever is very important because it means that you live for ever with God. This helps to comfort people and make them less frightened of death. In other religions, your time in Heaven is limited. Your soul only rests there for a short time until it returns to Earth to be reborn.

We have drunk
Soma, we have
become immortal.
We have gone to
the light, we have
found the gods.
What can hatred
and the malice of
mortal men
do to us now?

The Rig Veda

Millions
long for immortality who do not know what
to do with themselves on a rainy Sunday afternoon.

Susan Ertz
Anger in the Sky

A HELLISH TIME

OF course, living for ever would be great news in Heaven where life is an endless round of peace and happiness. No one would want such a good time to end. But it's not such fun if your soul ends up in Hell where instead of enjoying eternal bliss, any punishments you might have to suffer also last for ever! This was the fate awaiting Doctor Faustus, a man who sold his soul to Satan in exchange for a longer time on Earth. All was well until, one day, Satan came to claim his side of the bargain! Here Faustus is talking to himself, contemplating his fate. Don't worry if you don't understand all the words, you'll get the picture.

"Ah, Faustus,
Now hast thou but one bare hour to live,
And then thou must be damn'd perpetually!
Stand still, you ever-moving spheres of heaven,
That time may cease, and midnight never come;
Fair Nature's eye, rise, rise again, and make
Perpetual day; or let this hour be but
A year, a month, a week, a natural day,
That Faustus may repent and save his soul!"

Christopher Marlowe
Doctor Faustus

IMMORTALS GODS

MANY people believe that God or the gods are immortal. This means that they will live for ever, never growing old or dying. It is one of their special or magical powers which makes them different from people on Earth. But they sometimes need help to become immortal. Some gods drink a special potion or eat the fruits of long life, such as apples or peaches. There are many stories of envious humans desperately trying to find the elixir of immortality. For they wanted to live for ever, like the gods. The magical potion was never found, though some people keep on searching. For some people, living a good life on Earth is the only true way to win immortality.

SAYING GOODBYE

AROUND the world, people have different ways of saying goodbye to loved ones who have died. Deaths are often marked with special ceremonies at which prayers are said for the dead person's soul, to speed it on to the next world, and his or her body is buried or cremated. Not all ceremonies are religious. Instead of prayers and hymns, mourners may play the person's favorite piece of music or read out one of his or her best-loved poems.

Stop all the clocks, cut off the telephone,
Prevent the dog from barking with a juicy bone,
Silence the pianos and with muffled drum
Bring out the coffin, let the mourners come.

Let aeroplanes circle moaning overhead
Scribbling on the sky the message He is Dead,
Put crepe bows round the white necks of the
    public doves,
Let traffic policemen wear black cotton gloves.

He was my North, my South, my East and West,
My working week and my Sunday rest,
My noon, my midnight, my talk, my song;
I thought that love would last for ever: I was
    wrong.

The stars are not wanted now: put out every one;
Pack up the moon and dismantle the sun;
Pour away the ocean and sweep up the wood.
For nothing now can come to any good.

W. H. Auden

SACRED FIRE

WHEN a Hindu dies, the body is covered in an orange or white cloth and taken to be cremated, or burned. In India, it is placed on a platform of logs and sweet-smelling sandalwood. In other countries, it may be taken to the crematorium. While a priest chants from the sacred books, the person's eldest son, or another close male relative, lights the fire. Burning the body is a way of offering it up to Agni, god of fire, and of releasing the person's soul for rebirth.

FACING MAKKAH

MUSLIMS are always buried facing towards their holy city of Makkah. They are not allowed to be cremated because it is thought that, on the Last Day, their bodies will be brought back to life to be judged by Allah. The grave is marked with a simple stone.

FLOWERS AND FUNERALS

TODAY people often pay their respects at funerals by leaving gifts of flowers. This is a very old custom. An ancient grave found in Iraq contained the body of a man laid to rest about 60,000 years ago. Around his body, mourners had placed bunches of flowers – cornflowers, hollyhocks and grape hyacinths. In ancient times, people were also buried with food, clothes, tools, and jewelery, all the things they might need in the next world.

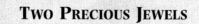

TWO PRECIOUS JEWELS

THERE was once a rabbi who had two young sons. He and his wife loved them very dearly. One day, tragedy struck and both sons died. The rabbi was not at home at the time as it was the Sabbath and he was teaching in the synagogue.

On his return, his wife greeted him with a question.

"Some time ago," she said, "a friend gave me two jewels to keep safe for him. Today, he wants them back. What shall I do?"

"Why, you must give them back, of course," replied the rabbi.

Then his wife took his hand and led him into the room where their two sons lay.

"These," she said, sadly, "these are the jewels I must return."

The rabbi was heartbroken, but through his tears, he remembered the words of the scriptures:

"The Lord has given and the Lord has taken away.
Blessed be the name of the Lord."

"I went to my grandma's funeral with my mother. It was very sad and my mother and auntie cried a lot. But lots of people said nice things about my grandma and that made me feel a bit better. We still have our lovely memories of her."

**John
aged 10**

MORE GOODBYES

It can be very frightening and upsetting when someone dies. You may find it difficult to express your feelings of sadness and hurt, or to talk about them to other people. Funerals and other ceremonies give people a chance to show and share their grief, to comfort each other, and to remember the happy times in the person's life.

THE BUDDHA AND THE MUSTARD SEED

One day, a woman called Kisagotami came to the Buddha. She was weeping because her only child had died.

"I beg you, Lord Buddha," she entreated, "Please give me some medicine to bring my child back to life."

The Buddha looked at Kisagotami with kindly eyes. He saw how unhappy she was. But he knew that no medicine could bring her dead child back to life.

"Go into town," he said to her, "and bring back a mustard seed, from a house where no one has died."

So Kisagotami hurried into town. She didn't think her task would be too hard. But wherever she went, the reply was the same. In every house she visited, someone had died. One family had lost their old grandfather; another woman had lost her husband.

Later that day, she returned to the Buddha.

Now she understood.

"Where is the mustard seed?" the Buddha asked.

Kisagotami smiled.

"'I see now that I am not alone in my sorrow," she said. "For death is part of life. It happens. Everything changes, and death touches everyone sooner or later."

A LONG SLEEP

SIKHS think of death as a long sleep, during which your soul rests before being reborn. Ultimately the aim is to stay with God and not be reborn. The most important prayer at a Sikh funeral is the Sohila, or evening prayer, which Sikhs say every night. It reminds them that death is like sleep. This is part of the prayer:

Know the reason why you are here.
Gather up your treasures under
the true Guru's guidance.
Turn your mind into God's home.
If God is always with you, you will
not be reborn.

SHINTO FUNERAL

AT a Shinto funeral in Japan, the dead person's name is written on two wooden tablets. One is placed in the grave; the other in the family's shrine at home. After 49 days, the wooden tablet is replaced with a tablet decorated with gold and becomes the focus of the family's prayers. Offerings of food and water are also given. In this way, the dead person's soul remains an important part of the family.

Apart from showing respect for a loved one, mourning clothes show other people that there has been a death in the family.

MARKS OF MOURNING

AT Christian funerals, mourners often wear black or dark clothes. This shows respect and matches the solemn occasion. But legend says black was first worn to protect people from being snatched by the dead person's ghost which hovered near the body. By wearing drab clothes, people hoped to blend into the crowd and avoid the ghost's unwelcome attention! In Hindu and Chinese beliefs, white is the color of mourning. In some African societies, it is red.

*Death is the close
of life's alarms
The watch light
on the shore
The clasping of
immortal arms
Of loved ones
gone before.*

**Engraving on a
Christian tombstone
in Canada**

*Though the color be fragrant
The flower will fall.
Who in this world of ours
Will last forever?*

Japanese poem

WAYS OF REMEMBERING

IN many cultures and beliefs, special ceremonies are held to remember a loved one who has died. Many are held every year, on the anniversary of the person's death. Some are large-scale events, marked by a whole religion or country. Others are smaller, more private times for family and friends.

YEAR'S TIME

EACH year, Jewish people remember a loved one's death. This anniversary is called *Yahrzeit*, or "year's time". On this day, the family light a special memorial candle which burns for twenty-four hours. This may be placed next to a photograph of the person. They also recite the *Kaddish* prayer (see below). Mourners always stand to say the Kaddish prayer and face towards Jerusalem, the Jews' holy city in Israel.

Blessed is he that cometh in the name of the Lord; Hosanna in the highest.

The Bible, Matthew 21:9

This is a Palm Sunday procession in Greece. Palm Sunday is the Sunday before Easter. It marks the start of Holy Week.

HOLY WEEK

EACH year, at Easter, Christians hold a week of festivals during which they remember how Jesus died on the cross and came back to life again. This belief in Jesus' new life is called the Resurrection. Easter is a very important time for Christians because it gives them hope of a new life with God. They mark it with special services in church to thank God for Jesus' life.

Do you know why people give chocolate eggs at Easter? It is because eggs are a reminder of new life. People also eat hot cross buns to remind them of the cross on which Jesus died.

FOOD FOR THE SOUL

IN Hindu families, the anniversary of a death is marked with a ceremony called *shraddha*. The family priest says prayers and offers rice balls and water to the dead person's soul to help it enjoy a better rebirth. Every year in autumn, a special shraddha is held which lasts for fifteen days. This is when people remember the last three generations of their family. In many homes at this time, men do not shave, or cut their nails or hair. The story on the next page tells how the custom began.

THERE was once a Hindu king called Karna. Outwardly, he was so devout that he liked to fast every day and give gifts of pure gold to the Brahmin priests. And he made very sure that everyone knew about it. When King Karna died, he went straight to Heaven where he was given a golden palace to live in, and nothing to eat or drink but gold, since giving away gold had been his only generous act in life. Finally, when he was starving with hunger, he asked to be allowed one last wish – to return to Earth for the great shraddha festival. His wish was granted. King Karna spent the whole two weeks of the festival giving away food to the hungry. He was so caught up in his task that he forgot to have a bath, shave, or wash his clothes. Afterwards, he returned to Heaven, and this time because of his great humility he had plenty of real food to eat!

May your eyesight return to the sun,
Your breath to the winds,
May your waters mingle with the ocean
And your earthly being become one with the earth.

A Hindu prayer

MORE MEMORIES

SOME people believe that the spirits of loved ones who have died watch over you and help you in times of trouble. So, it is very important to honor the spirits, and to look after their needs. If you forget or neglect them, they could turn nasty!

The Day of the Dead is a time for giving your friends and neighbors spooky gifts, like toy skulls and bones!

SPIRIT OFFERINGS

AT the festival of Ch'ing ming in China, people visit the graves of their ancestors to spring-clean them, and leave offerings of food and wine. Then the whole family enjoys a picnic by the graveside. It is a happy occasion, not a sad one. The sites of Chinese graves are carefully chosen to make sure that the soul rests peacefully. If the place is unlucky, the soul will be angry and take its revenge.

A WARM WELCOME

IN Japan, the O-bon festival in July is a time for welcoming the spirits of the dead back home. People light lamps to show them the way and place flowers on the family shrine. There is special food for them to eat and even entertainments. At the end of the festival, hundreds of tiny, sparkling lanterns are floated on lakes and rivers to see the spirits safely off again.

DAY OF THE DEAD

ON November 1 and 2 , Mexicans celebrate the Day of the Dead when the souls of the dead return briefly to Earth. Families clean their homes and set up tables of tortillas, chicken and hot chocolate for the souls to feast on. Unseen and unheard, the souls return to take up the essence of the food. Afterwards they return to their resting places and the family share the feast with friends.

TRICK OR TREAT?

THE 31 October is Hallowe'en, the evening before the Christian festival of All Saints or All Hallows. This developed from an ancient Celtic festival when the souls of the dead were said to come back to visit their homes. Bonfires were lit to scare off evil spirits. It is now the time for trick or treat when children knock on neighbors' doors and play tricks on those who do not give them a treat. This game started as a way to keep the Hallowe'en spirits happy. If you upset them, they would trick you for sure. If you like dressing up as a ghost or a ghoul, Hallowe'en is a great night for a party!

THE TALE OF JACK-O'-LANTERN

THE eerie light which sometimes dances over marshy land is known as Jack-o'-lantern. This is also the name of a spooky character in a Hallowe'en tale.

Jack was not afraid of anyone, not even of the devil himself. He even agreed to meet him at midnight, and the two of them struck a deal. The devil agreed to let Jack enjoy seven more years of fun before he came back to take his soul to Hell.

For seven years, Jack had a merry old time, doing exactly what he liked. But the devil had not forgotten him. As soon as the seven years were up, the devil appeared at Jack's door.

"Come in," said Jack. "I've been waiting for you. Before we go, just reach up to that shelf, would you, and get me down that hat."

The devil reached up and BANG! Jack nailed his hand to the wall.

"I'll let you go," he told the devil, "if you leave me alone for ever."

The devil promised.

But when Jack died, no one wanted his soul. Heaven didn't want him, neither did Hell.

"I'm not taking you," hissed the devil, and threw a ball of fire at him.

So Jack was left to wander the land, always with his fiery glow. He still works his mischief whenever he can, tricking travelers to follow him into marshy bogs. Don't ever go after him, if you should see him.

THE MAKING OF A CHARM

**From *Macbeth*
by William Shakespeare**

*Double, double, toil and trouble;
Fire burn, and cauldron bubble.*

*Fillet of a fenny snake,
In the cauldron boil and bake;
Eye of newt, and toe of frog,
Wool of bat, and tongue of dog,
Addder's fork, and blind-worm's
    sting,
Lizard's leg, and howlet's wing,
For a charm of powerful trouble,
Like a hell-broth, boil and bubble.*

*Double, double, toil and trouble;
Fire burn, and cauldron. bubble.*

Heavenly Beings

So if and when you get to Heaven, who will you meet there? Who or what lives in Heaven? Some people think that Heaven is the home of God or of a great spirit who watches over the world below. From high in the sky, he, or she, controls everything that happens on Earth. In other beliefs, Heaven is the home of many different gods and goddesses, and other holy beings such as saints and angels. Many people believe that, in Heaven, you will be reunited with others who have died before you. They might be members of your family or even your pets. Meeting up with your loved ones again will be one of the great joys of Heaven. Better still, in Heaven everyone will live together happily, with no more falling out or getting on each other's nerves!

LORDS OF HEAVEN

HAVE you ever been caught outside in a wild storm? Since ancient times, people have looked to the skies in wonder and awe. They believed that the heavens were the home of powerful gods whose actions caused day and night, the changing seasons and the weather. They worshiped these gods and showed them great respect. For it was they who brought the light, warmth, and life-giving rain which nourished all life on Earth.

This Ancient Egyptian painting shows Ra, the sun god, with a ram's head. The glowing circle between his horns represents the sun.

DAY AND NIGHT

THE Ancient Egyptians worshiped the Sun god, Ra. From dawn to dusk, Ra sailed across the sky in his golden boat. This was when the Sun shone and all was well. Each night, Ra traveled down into the underworld and darkness fell. People were so afraid of the dark that Ra made the Moon to light up the sky while he was away.

THE KITCHEN GOD

EVERY New Year, Chinese families traditionally worship Tsao Chun, the kitchen god. They hang his paper picture above the kitchen stove. The kitchen god decides your destiny, depending on how you behave. At New Year, he flies to Heaven to make his report. The day before, people spread honey around the picture's mouth to sweeten his tongue or make his mouth so sticky he cannot speak! Then the picture is burnt to speed him on his way to Heaven.

THUNDERSTRUCK

WOE betide when thunder and lightning stirred up the skies. This meant that the storm gods were angry. Many people in ancient times thought that thunder was the sound of the gods roaring with rage. Lightning was the sparks which flew from their weapons as they hurled them down from Heaven. The Hindu storm god was Indra, the warrior. He used his thunderbolt to kill his arch-enemy, a dragon called Vritra, who tried to capture the clouds from Indra.

THOR'S LOST HAMMER

THE Norse god of thunder and war was Thor. The Norse people described him as a huge, strong man with a bushy, red beard, and a fiery temper to match. Storms were thought to be caused by Thor hurling his great stone hammer at his enemies, the giants.

One day, in Asgard, home of the gods, Thor could not find his hammer. The other gods were worried too – without it they had nothing to fight the giants with. So they sent the god, Loki, disguised as a falcon, to fly off in search of it. He came back with news that the giant, Thrym, had stolen the hammer and buried it deep underground. He would only return it on one condition – that the beautiful goddess, Freyja, become his bride. Freyja was so angry she shook with rage. Then she burst into tears.

Luckily, one of the gods had a plan. They dressed Thor up in a wedding dress and veil, and sent him off to the land of the giants where a sumptous wedding feast was waiting. When the time came to bless the bride, the hammer was brought in and placed in the bride's lap. Thor seized his chance. He grabbed the hammer, struck Thrym to the ground and set off back to Asgard in great triumph.

HEAVENLY GODDESSES

THERE are many stories about all the gods and goddesses who live in Heaven. These stories were told to try to help people understand how the world worked and to show them the right way to live their lives on Earth.

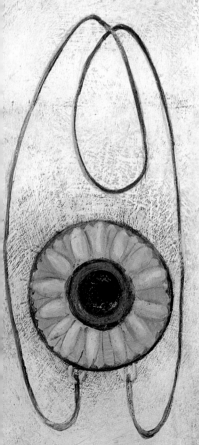

WHEN THE SUN WENT OUT

IN the Shinto religion, Amaterasu-o-Mikami, the 'heavenly shining one' is the Sun goddess, the greatest goddess of all. Legend tells how, one day, she quarreled with her brother, Susanoo, the sea god.

Susanoo had been banished to the underworld because of his terrible temper. Before he left, he went to visit his sister in Heaven. She was busy in the sacred weaving hall, making clothes for the gods.

Amaterasu prepared for a fight - she knew how fiery her brother could be. But, to prove his good intentions, Susanoo challenged her to a contest. If he could be the first to produce five sons, she would believe he meant well.

Amaterasu took her brother's sword and broke it in three. Each piece turned into a girl. Susanoo took his sister's necklace and smashed it into five pieces. Each piece turned into a boy. This meant that Susanoo had won! He began to celebrate.

"But it was my necklace," said Amaterasu. "So I won."

Susanoo was furious. In a dreadful rage, he picked up a pony and hurled it through the roof of the hall. Terrified, Amaterasu ran away and hid in a dark cave. And this is how the Sun went out and the world plunged into darkness. The crops died and evil spirits roamed the Earth, causing mischief and chaos.

In despair, the eight hundred gods met by the Heavenly River. How could they coax Amaterasu out of her cave? They thought and thought, and at last they came up with a plan. Outside the cave, they started to dance, laugh, and clap their hands until curious Amaterasu could stand it not longer. She peeked out to see what was going on.

Quick as a flash, one god grabbed her hand and pulled her out, while another stretched a magic rope across the cave door to stop her going back inside. Soon the Sun shone again, the crops grew and the evil spirits ran away. And the gods begged Amaterasu never to hide her shining face again.

QUEEN OF HEAVEN

THE gods and goddesses of ancient Greece were said to live on mighty Mount Olympus whose snow-capped summit soared up to Heaven. Zeus was king of the gods, and ruler of Heaven. His wife was the great goddess, Hera. Zeus and Hera often quarreled, making the sound you hear as thunder. As queen of the sky, Hera's symbol was a beautiful peacock. Its spangled feathers stood for the stars of Heaven.

GODDESS IN THE MOON

IN Chinese legend, a very beautiful goddess called Chang E lives on the Moon. Once, she and her husband were banished to Earth to live for a while as mortals. But Chang E was miserable and longed to return to Heaven. So she stole the elixir of eternal life and drank it all down, leaving none for her husband. Off she floated to the Moon. But when she got there, the Lord of Heaven turned her into an ugly, croaking toad to punish her for her foolishness. But he pitied her husband and let him back into Heaven. And later he showed Chang E mercy too. He turned her back into a goddess and let her live in the Palace of the Moon, where she still lives today.

A Shinto prayer
to Amaterasu

As you have blessed the emperor's reign
And made it long and lasting,
So I bow down my neck as a cormorant in search
of fish
To worship you and give you praise.

AMAZING ANGELS

IF someone described you as an angel, what do you think they meant? It's certain to be a compliment! Maybe you have done a good turn or a favor. In some religions, angels are believed to be heavenly beings, created by God from fire or light. They usually live in Heaven with God but are sometimes sent down to Earth to bring people messages about God's wishes or to perform other tasks, such as carrying our prayers up to Heaven.

'Praise be to God, Creator of the heavens and earth! He sends forth the angels as his messengers, with two, three or four pairs of wings. He multiplies his creatures according to his will. God has power over all things.'
The Qur'an, surah 35

SHINING ONES

IF you try to imagine an angel, you probably think of a beautiful creature with a halo and wings. A bright, sparkling light often shines around angels which some people think is a sign of God's power. Many ancient people thought that birds were the messengers of the gods, carrying dead people's souls to the other world. Later on, angels were given birds' wings so that they too could fly between Heaven and Earth.

The archangel Jibril

HEAVENLY VOICES

CHERUBIM are the angels which you often see on Christmas cards, playing a flute or a harp. But there are many other types of angels. Perhaps because of their beautiful voices Christian writers divided angels into three groups called choirs which circle around God's throne. In the most important are the Seraphim, Cherubim, and Thrones. Seraphim sing God's praises. Cherubim keep records of God's work. Thrones help God's wishes to be understood.

GOD'S MESSENGERS

YOU may have heard of the archangel Gabriel. He is important for Jews, Christians, and Muslims (who call him Jibril) as the angel who brings messages from God to Earth. In the Christian Bible, Gabriel appears to Mary and tells her that she will have a baby called Jesus. Jibril is sent by Allah to the Prophet Muhammad to give him the words of the Qur'an, the holy book of the Muslims.

Matthew, Mark, Luke and John,
Bless the bed that I lie on.
Four corners to my bed,
Four angels round my head.
One to watch and one to pray
And two to bear my soul away.
Traditional nursery rhyme

GUARDIAN ANGELS

SOME people believe that there are guardian angels who look after them from the day they are born. If you need help, simply ask your angel.

In Islam, everyone is believed to have two guardian angels, one sitting on their left shoulder and one on their right, to protect them from demons and evil spirits. But Muslims also believe their guardian angels record their good and bad deeds so that, when they die, they are judged accordingly and sent to Heaven or Hell.

Modern guardian angels are often thought to be the spirits of people close to us who have died. They watch over us and keep us safe from harm.

"Guardian angels stay with you throughout the night and give you nice dreams."
Catriona Brown
aged 8

53

MEETINGS WITH ANGELS

MANY **people claim to have seen an angel, or even to have been helped by one. Have you? Perhaps if something is troubling you, you could tell your guardian angel about it and they may be able to help you deal with your worry. There are many stories about people meeting angels, both a long time ago and more recently.**

SEEING AN ANGEL

AN old saying goes, "Be not afraid to have strangers in your house, for some thereby have entertained angels." This means that you should always make people welcome when they visit – one of them just might be an angel in disguise! Some people believe angels live all around us. You can't usually see them but they are there, watching over us always.

TALKING TO ANGELS

DID you know that you can talk to angels in their own language? If you want to call an angel to Earth, simply say, "Ils dialprt, soba upaah chis nanba zixlay dodsih." Then wait and see what happens. This angelic language was worked out in the sixteenth century by Queen Elizabeth I's astrologer, John Dee, and a medium called Edward Kelley. They based it on messages which they said had been given to them by angels.

MODERN ANGELS

IN our modern world, people such as doctors and nurses are often called angels because they look after others and try to make life better for them. Other modern angels might be people who care for hurt or unwanted animals, or who work for charities helping people in need. Can you think of anyone else whom you would count as an angel?

HOW MANY ANGELS?

IN the Middle Ages, people were fascinated by angels and had long debates about them. For example, they spent hours working out how many angels there were in Heaven. One person guessed at 266,613,336, exactly! Others tried to work out how many angels would fit on a pinhead. What do you think? One scholar said the answer was none because angels were more than 94 miles (150 km) high!

WHICH ANGEL?

OVER the centuries various angels have been associated with a particular attribute. Apart from the archangels, Michael the protector, Gabriel the messenger, and Raphael the healer, there are many other angels.

- Af (angel of anger)
- Arael (angel of birds)
- Rashiel (angel of earthquakes)
- Manna (angel of food)
- Poteh (angel of forgetfulness)
- Mumiah (angel of health)
- Rampel (angel of mountains)
- Israfel (angel of music)
- Matriel (angel of rain)
- Parasiel (angel of treasure)

"As a nurse, my job is to help people get better or to talk to them and comfort them when they're ill. If I can succeed at that, that is Heaven for me."

Sam Johnson
nurse

SAINTLY BEINGS

You might think saints lived long ago and have nothing to do with us today. But you often hear people saying, "You're a saint" when someone has done a kind deed. In Christian beliefs, saints are very good, holy people. Some have led very good or caring lives on Earth. Others have died for their faith. Some Christians when they pray ask the saints for their help and for God's help. They may also visit places associated with the saints. Some saints are said to look after certain people or things; for example, St Francis is the patron saint of animals. There are saintly beings in other religions too, pure, kindly people who seek to help others to lead better and more purposeful lives.

SAINT'S DAYS

MANY Christian saints have special days in the year on which they are remembered with special prayers. All the saints are honored on November 1, All Saints' Day. For many Christians, Mary, Jesus's mother, is their most important saint. She is sometimes described as the Queen of Heaven. This is a famous Christian prayer which speaks about Mary:

"Hail Mary, full of Grace, the Lord is with thee,
Blessed art thou amongst women,
and blessed is the fruit of thy womb, Jesus.
Holy Mary, Mother of God,
pray for us sinners, now
and at the hour of our death."

Mary's flower is a lily

BECOMING A SAINT

NEW saints are still being recognized in the Roman Catholic Church. But it's a very long process, sometimes taking several hundred years! The person needs to have led a very holy life, performed a miracle, or died for his or her beliefs. All this information is sent to Rome to be considered and thoroughly checked. A priest, called a "devil's advocate", is appointed to find any faults. If the person passes this test, he or she is "beatified" or blessed by the Pope, then later declared a saint. Very few people make the saintly grade!

"There was Mother Teresa who died a few days after Princess Diana died [in September 1997]. She only kept a few things - the clothes she wore and her Bible and she gave everything else away to other people and cared for them and that's why she went to Heaven."

Leila aged 7

HELPING OTHERS

SOME Buddhists worship saintly beings called *bodhisattvas*. These are perfect, enlightened beings who could enter *nirvana*. Instead they stay on Earth to help others gain enlightenment too. The bodhisattva, Avalokiteshvara, is worshiped in Tibet for his great kindness and compassion. In paintings he is often shown with a thousand arms. Each has an eye to show that Avalokiteshvara sees and helps everyone in trouble, no matter who they may be.

SUFI SAINTS

SUFI Muslims seek a loving, personal relationship with God. They sometimes use music, dancing and chanting to get closer to God. Each Sufi group has a master called a *shaykh* who is known for his saintly behavior. He is a teacher whose life has been so blessed by God that he can pass on God's blessings to others. Among the most famous Sufis are the Whirling Dervishes of Turkey. They perform spectacular spinning dances.

Think, O think with a quiet mind of Avalokiteshvara, that pure being; he is a protector, a refuge, a recourse in death, disaster and calamity.

The Lotus Sutra

Getting to Heaven

WHERE is Heaven and how do you get there? Some people believe that Heaven is a mysterious place above the Earth, somewhere far away in time and space. Perhaps it was placed so high in the sky to show how important it was. From these lofty heights, among the sun, moon, and stars, the gods could look down on Earth and watch over people's lives. There were many ways of getting to Heaven. Your soul might have to cross a fast-flowing river or a narrow bridge, or climb up a steep ladder. The journey was often difficult and dangerous, filled with obstacles to overcome, but if you believed in Heaven strongly enough and had led a good life on Earth, you'd be sure to get to Heaven eventually.

HOW THE WORLD BEGAN

MOST people are fascinated by how the world was formed. It is such an enormous idea. Since ancient times, people have told stories to try to explain how the world began, and how Heaven and Earth came to be. Many tell how the gods created the world and everything in it, including the first people. Sometimes Earth was made as a copy of Heaven, to mirror the gods' home in the sky, and people were created in the image of the gods. Sometimes a new world was formed from an egg which hatched to reveal Heaven and Earth.

RAINBOW BRIDGE

THIS is the Shinto story of creation. In the beginning, the world was shaped like an egg. The top was Heaven and the bottom was Earth. The god, Izanagi, and the goddess, Izanami, stood on the Floating Bridge of Heaven which glimmered and gleamed with all the colors of the rainbow. They took a long, jeweled spear and began to stir the bottom part of the egg. Soon an island appeared – the first dry land on Earth. They liked the island so much, they went to live on it, in a beautiful palace whose roof reached up to Heaven.

UPSIDE-DOWN WORLD

IN an African legend, the Earth was divided into two parts by an ocean. Above was the land of the living which rose up like a mountain. Below was the world of the dead, an upside-down version of the land of the living, with upside-down villages, rivers, and hills. You reached this land through a porcupine burrow. Here people slept by day and came out at night. Above the Earth, divided from it by a rainbow, was Heaven, the home of the gods.

SPIDERS AND SHELLS

A story from the South Pacific tells how, when the world began, there was nothing but sea and a giant spider. One day, Spider found a giant clamshell. She opened the shell just wide enough to slip inside. But it was dark because there was no moon or sun and much too small to stand up in. Spider hunted about for two magic snails, one big and one small. Then she prized the clamshell open again. The top half became the sky; the bottom half the Earth. She placed the two snails in the sky, the bigger one as the shining sun, the smaller one as the pale face of the moon.

THE SEVEN DAYS

IN the Jewish and Christian religions, the story of creation is told in Genesis, the first book of the Hebrew Bible.

In the beginning, God created the heavens and Earth. He made light, and separated the light from the darkness to give the first day and the first night.

On the second day, God made the sky and called it Heaven. On the third day, he created dry land and the seas, and made grass, trees, and plants grow from the Earth. On the fourth day, he made the sun, moon, and stars to shine down on the Earth. And he divided up time into days, years, and seasons. On the fifth day, God created fish and whales, and filled the sky with birds. On the sixth day, he made all the creatures on land. And he created the first man and first woman and gave them a beautiful garden to live in.

On the seventh day, the heavens and Earth were finished and filled with life. God rested and made this a holy day on which no work should be done.

Heaven is like an egg, and the Earth is like a yolk of an egg.

The Sayings of Chang Heng

BOATS AND BRIDGES

HAVE you ever walked across a rickety bridge over a river? It can be scary but thrilling, and you feel a great sense of achievement when you reach the other side. Some people imagine that, when you die, your soul goes on a journey between Heaven and Earth. On the way you might have to prove your worthiness by passing a test, crossing a river or walking over a narrow bridge to reach your heavenly destination. Will you make it? The answer is yes - if you've led a good life on Earth. If not, you may have a long and very rocky road ahead of you!

Somewhere
over the rainbow
Way up high
There's a land that I
heard of
Once in a lullaby.
Somewhere over the rainbow
Skies are blue
And the dreams that you dare
to dream
Really do come true.

E.Y. Harburg
The Wizard of Oz

BRIDGE TO HEAVEN

THE Zoroastrian faith began in Persia (modern-day Iran) about 3,000 years ago. Its greatest teacher was the prophet Zoroaster. Zoroastrians believe that a bridge of reckoning leads from Earth to Heaven. For the good, it appears as wide as nine spears laid end to end. For the wicked, it seems as narrow as a razor blade. When you die, your soul has to cross the bridge, led by your conscience. If you've led a good life, your conscience is clear and leads you safely across the bridge into Heaven. If you've been wicked, your guilty conscience throws you off the bridge into the House of the Lie, a type of Hell.

ON A KNIFE EDGE

IN traditional Muslim beliefs, the way to Paradise, and Hell, is believed to be across a bridge called al-Sirat which is "thinner than a hair and sharper than a sword" and spans the valley of Hell. True believers cross quickly, helped by the angels who hold them up by their hair. Wicked people take longer, depending on how bad they have been. The worse you have been, the longer it takes. Some take 25,000 years to cross, all the time being burned by flames coming from Hell.

PAYING THE FERRYMAN

THE Ancient Greeks believed that the souls of the dead traveled by boat across the River Styx to an underground kingdom called Hades. The river marked the boundary between the land of the living and the Underworld. Dead people were buried with coins in their mouths to pay the ferryman to take them across. They also took honeycakes to feed to Cerberus, the terrifying three-headed dog which guarded the entrance to Hades.

A ROCKY ROAD

IN some parts of Europe, dead people were buried with their boots on so that they could cross Whinnymuir, a mythical land covered with prickly gorse, brambles, and thorns. It led to a bridge "no broader than a thread" which crossed over to Heaven. Mourners burned candles so that the dead could see their way.

There is a bridge between time and Eternity; and this bridge is Atman, the Spirit of Humankind. Neither day nor night cross that bridge, nor old age, nor death, nor sorrow. Evil or sin cannot cross that bridge, because the world of the Spirit is pure. This is why when this bridge has been crossed, the eyes of the blind can see, wounds are healed, and the sick become whole. To one who goes over that bridge, the night becomes like day, because in the world of the Spirit there is a Light which shines for ever.

The Chandogya Upanishad

Spiders' Webs, Sacred Fire

There are many imaginative ideas about how you can cross between Heaven and Earth. In African legend, the gods came down to Earth on a spider's web. In Ancient Egypt, the souls of the dead climbed up a ladder of sunbeams or traveled along the Milky Way. A Tibetan story tells how the first kings descended to Earth on a magic rope and, when their reigns were over, they climbed back up to Heaven again.

I give you the end of a golden string.
Only wind it into a ball,
It will lead you to Heaven's gate
Built in Jerusalem's wall.

William Blake
Heaven's Gate

Jacob's Ladder

The Hebrew Bible tells the story of Jacob who saw a ladder reaching up into Heaven. Jacob was forced to leave his home because he had stolen his older brother Esau's inheritance, and now Esau wanted to kill him. When night fell, Jacob lay down on the ground, with a rock for his pillow, and fell asleep. In his dreams, he saw a great ladder with its foot on the ground and its top in Heaven, and angels climbing up and down. At the top of the ladder stood God. He told Jacob that the place he slept in was his, to keep for himself and his children. When Jacob woke up, he remembered his dream, saying, "This is surely the house of God, and this is the gate of Heaven."

SACRED FIRE

WHEN Hindus die, their bodies are burnt, or cremated. Also on special occasions, such as weddings, offerings are thrown into a fire. This is because fire is sacred. It is worshiped as the great god, Agni, who carries messages between Heaven and Earth. So the fire carries the dead person's soul, and the offerings, up towards the heavens. Agni is often shown with flame-red skin, yellow eyes and black clothes, and holding a burning spear.

BIRDS AND BEES

SOME people think that when you die, birds carry your soul up to Heaven. In many beliefs, a mighty eagle soars through the skies to Paradise. The Aztecs believed that the souls of brave warriors turned into eagles who were placed on guard around the sun. Early Christians believed that bees were God's messengers and their buzzing a song of praise. It was very unlucky to kill a bee.

"When you die, your body stays here but your soul climbs up an invisible ladder to Heaven."

**Ranjit
aged 7**

HEAVENLY PLACES

Do you have a favorite place? Somewhere that makes you feel happy and peaceful? It might be near the sea, by a riverbank or somewhere hidden away in the countryside. Many people have special places on Earth, where the beauty of their surroundings helps them to feel closer to Heaven. These places are like meeting points between Heaven and Earth. Some are natural; others have been made by people.

HEAVENLY LINES

SOME people believe that the Earth's sacred places are linked together by invisible lines of energy. These are called ley lines. Ancient people located many of their temples, shrines, holy wells, and stone circles along these lines and used them to guide them from one place to another. Ley lines can stretch for hundreds of miles across the countryside. Some people think they cover the whole Earth. The ancient stone circle of Stonehenge in Wiltshire, England, was built at the point where two ley lines meet, a particularly powerful place.

WIND AND WATER

IF you're moving into a new house, make sure that it's positioned according to the ancient rules of *Feng Shui*. If things go wrong, it could be because your house has bad Feng Shui. Even moving the furniture can help! In Chinese, Feng Shui means "wind and water." For a happy life, you need to choose a house where these two things are in balance. This will allow *Ch'i*, the invisible life force, to flow freely and bring Heaven into your home.

CROSSING OVER

FOR Hindus, *tirthas* are sacred crossing places between Heaven and Earth. The holiest is Varanasi, a bustling city on the banks of the sacred River Ganges. Hindus believe that bathing in the Ganges will wash away their sins. At Varanasi, its water is particularly holy and powerful. More auspicious still is to die in the city and be cremated on the river bank. Then you will achieve moksha. According to legend, Varanasi was the place chosen by the great god, Shiva, to be his home on Earth. Millions of pilgrims visit the city every year.

At Stonehenge the stones were very carefully placed to be at the meeting point of two ley lines and to catch the rays of the sun.

HOW THE GANGES FELL FROM HEAVEN

KING Bhagiratha was a very holy man who spent many years worshiping the gods. To reward the king for his devotion, the gods gave him a magnificent horse which became his pride and joy. Then, one day, demons stole the horse and carried it off to the underworld. Now, Bhagiratha had 60,000 sons who set off to find the lost horse. They dug a huge hole deep down into the Earth but were burned to ashes by the heat and flames.

The King was heartbroken. There was only one thing that could save them.

"Lord Shiva," he prayed. "Let the river of Heaven flow to Earth and bring my sons back to life."

Shiva took pity on the King and ordered the Ganges to fall from Heaven. To cushion its fall, the great god caught the river in his long tangled hair. Otherwise it would have crushed the Earth. Then he let it flow, very gently and slowly, down from the mountains, across the plains, to the sea and down into the underworld. There its sacred waters brought King Bhagiratha's sons back to life.

God made the rivers to flow.
They feel no weariness, they cease not
from flowing. They fly swiftly like birds
in the air.

The Rig Veda

SACRED MOUNTAINS

BECAUSE of their awe-inspiring height and size, mountains play a special part in people's beliefs about Heaven. With towering peaks that rise high into the sky, they were thought to be the closest points to Heaven, a link between Heaven and Earth. The gods were believed to live on their summits, watching over the Earth below. By climbing a mountain, many people hoped to get closer to Heaven. And if you've ever stood on top of a mountain, with clear, blue sky above and around you, you'll know exactly what they mean!

HOME OF THE GODS

THE Himalayas are the world's highest mountains, stretching for 1500 miles (2400 km) across northern India, Pakistan, Tibet, Nepal, and Bhutan. They are sacred to Buddhists and Hindus alike. Among them stands Mount Kailash, worshiped by Hindus as the home of the god Shiva and his wife Parvati. Pilgrims believe that walking around the foot of the mountain, a tough three-day trek on foot, will wipe away their sins and bring them closer to Heaven.

BETWEEN HEAVEN AND EARTH

HINDUS and Jains also believe that Mount Kailash is the legendary Mount Meru which marks the center of the universe, and whose summit links Heaven and Earth. According to legend, Mount Meru has slopes of gleaming gold, studded with precious rubies, crystals, and lapis lazuli, and covered with magic wishing trees. The gods sit on its summit to discuss their plans for the world.

MOUNTAIN OF MOSES

Mount Sinai in Egypt is sacred to both Jews and Christians. It is also called Jebel Musa, the mountain of Moses. The Hebrew Bible tells how Moses was summoned to the top of the mountain where God appeared as a blazing fire and gave Moses the Ten Commandments, ten important laws for people to follow in their lives. Today, thousands of pilgrims climb the mountain to follow in Moses's footsteps.

In Ancient Greece, Mount Olympus was the home of the gods.

Olympus, the abode of the Gods, that stands fast forever. Neither is it shaken by winds nor ever wet with rain, nor does snow fall upon it, but the air is outspread clear and cloudless, and over it hovers a radiant whiteness.

Homer
The Odyssey

A lot of us found faith up there. We were trespassing on sacred ground. I only hoped the mountain would forgive the steps I chopped in her. The higher we went, the more we could hear her voice fighting with the wind.

Sherpa Tenzing
The first man, with Sir Edmund Hillary, to climb Mount Everest in the Himalayas.

JOURNEYS TO HEAVEN

OR some people, going on holiday is a special journey. It is a time to refresh yourself and step away from the cares of everyday life. Each year, millions of people make special journeys, called pilgrimages, to holy places around the world. These might be buildings, such as temples or tombs, or natural places, such as sacred rivers or mountains. There are many reasons for undertaking such a journey. It might be to pray for something special, like good health, or to thank the gods for making wishes come true. For some people, simply being there is enough. It helps them to feel closer to Heaven.

STONE OF HEAVEN

USLIMS hope to make a pilgrimage to Makkah, in Saudi Arabia, at least once in their lives. This was the birthplace of the Prophet Muhammad and is the holiest city in Islam. The pilgrimage is called the *Hajj* and is one of the Five Pillars, or duties, of Islam. First the pilgrims dress in plain white clothes to show that they are all equal in Allah's eyes. Then they walk seven times around the sacred Ka'ba, a cube shaped shrine, said to have been built at Allah's command. On the last circuit, they try to touch or kiss a famous black stone, set in one corner. It is believed to have fallen from Heaven.

Let all men make the pilgrimage. They will come to you on foot and on the backs of swift camels from every distant quarter ... Let them put on clean clothes, make their vows, and circle the Ancient House. Such is God's commandment. He that reveres the sacred rites of God shall fare better in the sight of his Lord.

The Qur'an, surahs 26-31

70

The Western Wall

WALL OF PRAYERS

THE Western Wall in Jerusalem is the holiest place in the world for Jews. It is all that is left of the great Temple, destroyed in the year 70CE. Pilgrims gather in front of the wall to pray. God's presence is thought to rest in the wall so some people write their prayers on slips of paper and place them in cracks in the wall so that they reach God.

HOLY BONES

THE cathedral of Santiago de Compostela in Spain is one of the holiest Christian shrines. According to legend, this is the burial place of St James, one of Jesus's disciples. Pilgrims worship in the majestic cathedral built over St James's tomb. Since the Middle Ages, pilgrims have traveled to Santiago along ancient routes from France. Some still wear the traditional dress of a cape, and a curling felt cap decorated with scallop shells, the symbol of St. James, and carry a long staff.

TEMPLE OF ENLIGHTENMENT

FOR Buddhists, places linked to events in the Buddha's life have a special meaning. Each year, thousands of pilgrims flock to Bodh Gaya in India, the place where the Buddha gained enlightenment. There they honor the golden statue of the Buddha inside the sacred Mahabodhi Temple. Nearby grows a bodhi tree, said to be descended from the very tree under which the Buddha sat. Buddhists believe that going on a pilgrimage brings them merit which will help them enjoy a better rebirth.

SPECIAL BUILDINGS

A Christian cathedral

Do you have a favorite building? Somewhere that is special to you? It might be your home where you feel safe and secure. It might be your bedroom where you relax after a long day at school, chat to your friends, or listen to your favorite music. Religions have many special buildings. These are places where people can worship, learn about their faith, or simply sit quietly and think about God. Many sacred buildings are very beautiful to help lift people's spirits to Heaven and their prayers up to God.

SHAPED LIKE A CROSS

SACRED buildings are often built in a particular way which has a special meaning for worshipers. Many Christian churches are built in the shape of a cross. This reminds people that Jesus died on a cross. Inside, the altar stands at the eastern end, pointing in the direction of the rising sun which is a symbol of Jesus' resurrection (see p.13). Many churches have tall steeples or pointed spires which reach upwards to Heaven. They are places where Christians feel close to God.

DOOR OF THE GURU

SIKHS meet to worship in a building called a gurdwara. The word gurdwara means "door of the Guru." It is the place where the *Guru Granth Sahib*, the Sikhs' holy book is kept. The *Guru Granth Sahib* is a collection of hymns and prayers which guides Sikhs. It is treated with great respect. In the gurdwara, it is placed on a throne, like a king, to show how precious it is.

"I like the Cathedral, it's a bit like a castle only peaceful and quiet with lovely pictures and sometimes we sing and it echoes all around . . . it's a nice feeling."

Bill
aged 6

HOUSE OF GOD

A *mandir*, or temple, is a holy place where Hindus go to worship. Hindus believe that the mandir is God's home on Earth. Each mandir is dedicated to a god or goddess who represents God's presence. A sacred image of the god or goddess stands in the inner sanctum, the holiest part of the mandir. Hindus visit the mandir to pray and to have a *darshana*, or sight, of the image. They offer fruit, sweets, and flowers in return for God's blessing.

MIRROR OF NATURE

Some mandirs are small and simple. Others are large and grand. Traditional mandirs are built according to ancient rules of design. Each part of the building has a special meaning. The marble spires represent the sacred mountains of the gods which form a link between Heaven and Earth. The huge dome above the inner sanctum is the arch of the sky, or Heaven, from which God sends divine inspiration.

"When I go to the mandir, it clears my soul and I feel good. It is a place where time stops and your mind becomes still. In the mandir, I feel that I can see God and that I can feel God."

**Usha Patel
aged 12**

A Hindu mandir

WAYS OF WORSHIP

HERE are many ways of showing how much you love or care for someone. You might buy them a present, send a card, or give them a hug or a kiss. In the same way, people use different means to show their love and devotion for God. They say prayers, sing hymns and songs, give gifts or offerings, and read passages from their sacred books. These are sent soaring into Heaven with their hopes, fears, and dreams.

God's light is found in houses which he has allowed to be built in his name. In them, morning and evening, his praise is sung by men whom neither trade nor profit can divert from remembering him, from offering prayers, or from giving alms.

The Qur'an, surah 24

MUSLIM PRAYERS

MUSLIMS pray five times a day, in the morning, three times during the day and in the evening. This is one of the Five Pillars, or duties, of Islam. When they pray, they turn in the direction of the holy city of Makkah. Muslims believe that they can worship Allah anywhere but many visit a mosque to pray. The mosque has a small arch, the mihrab, in one wall to show the direction of Makkah.

These Muslims are praying in a mosque in India. Prayers are a very important part of Muslim worship. In their prayers, Muslims thank Allah for being able to worship him.

THE HOLY ARK

THE most important place in a Jewish synagogue is the Holy Ark. This is a cupboard at the front of the synagogue where the scrolls of the Torah are kept. The scrolls are taken out of the Ark for reading during services in the synagogue. The word Torah means "Books of Teaching." This is the first and holiest part of the Hebrew Bible. Jews believe that the Torah teaches them how God wants them to live and that God gave the Torah to Moses on Mount Sinai, thousands of years ago.

The angels came a-mustering,
A-mustering, a-mustering,
The angels came a-clustering
Around the sapphire throne.

A-questioning of one another,
Of one another, of one another,
A-questioning each one his brother
Around the sapphire throne.

Pray who is he, and where is he,
And where is he, and where is he,
Whose shining casts - so fair is he -
A shadow on the throne?

Pray, who has up to heaven come,
To heaven come, to heaven come,
Through all the circles seven come,
To fetch the Torah down?

'Tis Moses up to heaven come,
To heaven come, to heaven come,
Through all the circles seven come,
To fetch the Torah down!

Traditional Jewish song

QUIET MEDITATION

MEDITATION is a very important part of Buddhist practice. It means training your mind to concentrate on positive thoughts and feelings. Buddhists believe that this will bring them closer to enlightenment. Meditating takes lots of hard practice. It isn't easy to clear your mind of all the thoughts buzzing around inside it. It can be helpful to count or repeat a word. Find a quiet place to sit, close your eyes, and try it. Don't forget to breathe calmly and evenly.

AT HOME

IN many religions, people also worship quietly at home or say their prayers in private. Even if you are not a religious person, taking a few moments out of every day to sit quietly and gather your thoughts is often a good thing. You might be surprised at how quickly the day's problems and worries seem to grow less or even disappear!

SHAMANS AND SPIRITS

SOME people believe that their lives are ruled by good and evil spirits. These spirits have power over life and nature, and can cause illness and death. In times of trouble, people ask the spirits for help. But how do they reach them? In some cultures, a type of priest called a *shaman* forms the link between Heaven and Earth. In a deep, sleep-like trance, his soul flies to the spirit world, high up in the sky or under the ground, and speaks to the spirits on people's behalf. Shamans are found in Siberia, North and South America, Australia, and South-east Asia.

RATTLES AND DRUMS

To reach the world of the spirits, the shaman falls into a trance, like a deep, deep sleep. Some shamans take drugs or alcohol to help them. Others dance or listen to the beating of a drum or rattle. The repetitive, rhythmical thump-thump-thump sound has a powerful effect. It's a bit like listening to a crowd applauding at a rock concert or football game. It makes you feel light-headed despite yourself.

A SHAMAN'S POWER

A shaman is like a cross between a priest, a magician, and a doctor, who is believed to have extraordinary powers and wisdom. If a person is ill, the shaman seeks out and defeats the evil spirits which are thought to cause the sickness. In places where people live by hunting or farming, the shaman asks the spirits to send plenty of animals or good weather for the harvest. Some shamans guide the souls of the dead to the spirit world. Some have the gift of seeing into the future.

SHIFTING SHAPE

SOME shamans are thought to turn into animals for their journey to the spirit world. This is called "shape-shifting." In South America, the shaman takes the form of a jaguar, the most powerful spirit in the forest. He wears a jaguar skin and a necklace of jaguar teeth, as symbols of strength. Among some Native North Americans, the grizzly bear is sacred. There the shaman dresses in a grizzly bear skin, and grunts, growls, and shuffles as he dances like a grizzly bear.

BECOMING A SHAMAN

TRAINING to be a shaman is very hard, and only a very few people have the gift. First you must show you are strong enough, in mind and body, to deal with the spirit world. This might mean spending a long time alone, without sleeping, eating, or drinking. Then it is believed the spirits may appear and call you. In Australia, a young shaman goes to a cave and falls into a deep sleep or trance. In his dreams, the spirits come and take away his old body but replace it with a new, better one. They also give him a supply of magic crystals. When he wakes up he is reborn as a shaman. The crystals contain the power of Baiame, the great spirit. They help the shaman fly up to Heaven.

Under the white sky,
Over the white cloud;
Under the blue sky,
Over the blue cloud:
Rise up to the sky, bird!
Siberian shaman

Skin-covered drum,
Fulfil my wishes,
Like flitting clouds, carry me
Through the lands of dusk
And below the leaden sky,
Sweep along like wind
Over the mountain peaks!
Siberian shaman's poem

SPIRIT JOURNEYS

STORIES about the shaman's journey to the world of the spirits say it is often long and dangerous. There are many obstacles to be overcome, as the shaman battles with the evil spirits which cause sickness and death. If the shaman has the power to control the spirits, all will be well. But if the evil spirits are too strong and overcome the shaman, he may never return from his journey.

"The great sea has set me in motion
Set me adrift.
Moving me as the weed moves in a river.
The arch of the sky and mightiness of storms
Have moved the spirit within me,
Till I am carried away
Trembling with joy."

Inuit shaman

SEARCH FOR THE SEA GODDESS

IN Inuit society, it is believed that the shaman's soul must travel to the bottom of the sea to speak to the sea spirit, Sedna, the keeper of the seals and other sea mammals. Seals are very important for the Inuit who eat their meat and make their skins into clothes. At times when seals are scarce, the shaman seeks out Sedna and asks for her help. It is a dangerous time. First he must dodge three deadly stones which try to crush him, then step over a fierce dog which guards the entrance to Sedna's home. Then he must comb and stroke her hair and talk to her kindly, to please her for the sea goddess has a terrible temper!

Black Elk Speaks

BLACK ELK was a famous Native North American (Sioux) shaman, or holy man, who was born in 1863. From his first meeting with the spirits at the age of five, he made many soul journeys which changed his life. This is the story of one of them.

As a young boy, Black Elk was in his tepee when he heard a voice calling, "It is time, now they are calling you." He looked out but there was no one there. Next day, Black Elk fell ill. As he lay in his tepee, he saw two men, holding long, flaming spears. "Hurry!" they said. "Come! Your Grandfathers are calling you!"

Then Black Elk began a long journey. He stepped outside and was carried off by a little cloud, up into the blue skies. Then Black Elk was standing with the two strangers, in the middle of a great white plain. Twelve magical horses came galloping past, lightning flashing from their manes. Then the clouds formed the shape of a giant tepee, with a rainbow as its open door. Through the door, Black Elk saw six men sitting in a row. They were old men, like the hills, like the stars. They were the Grandfathers, the Powers of the World.

The oldest man spoke kindly to Black Elk. "Come right in," he said. "And do not fear. Your Grandfathers have called you here to teach you."

They gave Black Elk a wooden cup of water, representing the power of life, a bow with the power to destroy, a herb for healing, and a bright red stick which sprouted like a Tree of Life. Then they led Black Elk through the heavens where he had four extraordinary visions. In them, he saw the fate and future of his people as their land and animals were taken from them, and they were left weak and afraid. Black Elk knew he must use his powers to help his people. He began to sing:

"A good nation I will make live.
This the nation above has said.
They have given me the power
to make over."

Black Elk found himself riding a beautiful black stallion that ran as fast as the wind. It carried him to the center of the world. There he stood on the highest mountain, and looked all around. And he saw more than he could tell, and understood more than he saw. In the middle of it all, he saw a great tree which sheltered all the children of the world beneath its huge branches.

When Black Elk returned to the Grandfathers' tepee, there was great rejoicing. But it was time now for him to go home. Far below, he could see his own tepee and his mother and father inside. They were bending over a sick boy who was himself. And, as he entered the tepee, the sick boy sat up. But his mother and father did not know how far away from them he had been.

Ancient Heavens

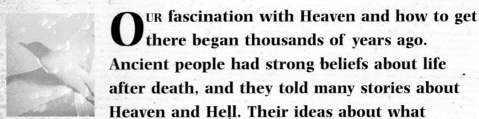

OUR fascination with Heaven and how to get there began thousands of years ago. Ancient people had strong beliefs about life after death, and they told many stories about Heaven and Hell. Their ideas about what Heaven might be like often reflected the things they held most dear or important in their own societies. For example, people who made their living by farming saw Heaven as a place full of lush fields and fine crops. For people who prided themselves on fighting, Heaven was a place reserved for the bravest warriors. Do you think your own life is pretty heavenly? Are you happy with where and how you live? If so, you might hope that Heaven will be very much like your life is now. Many ancient people hoped for the same. They believed that Heaven would be just like Earth, only many, many times better.

BATTLE IN HEAVEN

Towards the end of the eighth century CE, bands of sea-faring raiders from Scandinavia, known as the Vikings, began to plunder the coasts of northern Europe. The Vikings were brave, fearless warriors, striking terror wherever they went. At first, they raided churches and monasteries for their treasure. Later, they looted towns. For Viking warriors, courage, honor, and glory in battle were all important, a belief which strongly affected their view of Heaven.

THE LAST BATTLE

THE Vikings believed that, at the end of time, there would be a last great battle called Ragnarok, meaning "the doom of the gods." The battle would be fought between the gods (the forces of good) and the giants (the forces of evil). The souls of the dead warriors from Valhalla would fight on the side of the gods. In the battle, most of the gods would be killed. But two gods and two humans would survive to build a new and happier world.

VALHALLA

To die in battle was the greatest honor a Viking warrior could hope for. According to legend, the souls of dead heroes were snatched from the battlefield by fierce female warriors, called the Valkyries. They took the souls to Asgard, land of the gods, to live in Valhalla, also known as the "Hall of the Slain". This was a magnificent hall belonging to Odin, king of the gods, and god of war and death.

Valhalla was said to have walls of gleaming gold and a roof of shining shields, held up by rafters of golden spears. The warriors' souls entered one of Valhalla's hundreds of doors, each wide enough for eight hundred warriors to pass through. By day, the warriors rode out to fight. At night, they returned to the hall of Valhalla for a sumptuous feast, any battle wounds magically healed. In the mythical Valhalla this cycle of fighting and eating lasted for all eternity.

At the festival of Up-Helly-Aa, the people of Shetland in Scotland relive their Viking past. They burn a model of a Viking longboat to represent the funeral pyre of an important Viking chief.

THE TREE OF LIFE

IN Viking beliefs, the universe was split into three levels, held together by the roots of a gigantic ash tree. At the top was Asgard, a heavenly place where the gods lived. Below was Midgard, the middle world of humans. A rainbow bridge linked Heaven (Asgard) and Earth (Midgard). Around Midgard lay a mighty ocean, ringed by a huge serpent. On the lowest level were the lands of the dead, a dark, icy place called Niflheim, and Muspellheim, the land of fire. Asgard was not a heaven for everyone. Only the souls of Viking chieftains or warriors were allowed to enter. Other people languished in the lands of the dead.

Odin is called All-father, because he is the father of the gods. He is also called Valfather because his chosen sons are all those who die in battle. Valhalla is for them.

Snorri
Prose Edda

THE FIELD OF REEDS

The Ancient Egyptians saw earthly life as a dream, over and gone in a flash. Then your soul went on to enjoy a better life for all eternity in the Next World. This was a happy, heavenly place somewhere far away to the west. It was sometimes called the Field of Reeds. It was very similar to the actual land of Egypt, complete with fields, canals, dry dusty desert, and even its own heavenly version of the great River Nile. But it was even better and more beautiful. No wonder people had no fear of going there when they died!

THE FEATHER OF TRUTH

Before they could reach the Field of Reeds, the Ancient Egyptians believed that their souls had to pass a series of tests. First they had to cross the River of Death, then pass through the Twelve Gates, guarded by serpents. Finally, their deeds in life were judged by Osiris, god of the dead, in his Hall of Judgement. Here the dead person's heart was weighed against an ostrich feather, the symbol of truth. (This is shown in the picture below.) If the heart and feather balanced out, it meant the person had led a good life on Earth and could go to Heaven. But if your heart tipped the scales, you were gobbled up by a monster!

THE BOOK OF THE DEAD

IF you go on a long journey, do you take a map or a guidebook with you to help you find your way? The Ancient Egyptians did just the same. To help the dead find their way to Heaven, they carved spells and hymns on their tomb walls or wrote them down on papyrus scrolls which were placed inside their coffins. These texts became known as the *Book of the Dead*, a type of guidebook to the afterlife.

SAVING YOUR SOUL

YOU might have seen mummies in scary horror films or on display in a museum. But do you know what they really are? The Egyptians believed that everyone had three souls. For these to survive in the Next World, bodies had to be preserved and not left to rot. This is why they invented mummification. A dead body was packed in natron salt to dry it out, wrapped in strips of cloth, then placed in a coffin. And it worked so well that some mummies have lasted, almost intact, right up to the present day.

PATH TO THE SUN

THE mummies of some Egyptian kings, or pharaohs, were laid to rest in huge pyramid tombs. The Great Pyramid of Giza, built for King Khufu about 4,600 years ago, was one of the Seven Wonders of the World. The pharaoh's body was taken to the pyramid by barge, together with the objects he might need in the Next World. These included food, clothes, furniture, and even small statues of servants to wait on him in the afterlife. The pyramid's steep slanting sides represented the sun's rays. The pharaoh's soul was thought to walk up them to join the sun god in Heaven.

None comes back from there
That he may tell us how they fare;
That he may tell us of their fortunes,
That he may content our heart,
Until we too depart
To the place where they have gone.

Song of the Harpist

CROSSING THE RIVER

In Ancient Greek and Roman beliefs, an underground kingdom, called the Underworld or Hades, awaited the souls of the dead. It was ruled by Pluto (whom the Romans called Dis), the god of the dead. Hades was not seen as a heaven or hell but as a dull, rather gloomy place where all people went when they died, regardless of who they were or what they had done in life. What happened to them once they reached Hades, however, did depend on their past behavior on Earth.

PAYING THE FERRYMAN

THE ancient Greeks and Romans believed that when a person died, his or her soul was guided to Hades by the god Hermes. A mythical river, called the Styx, marked the boundary between the land of the living and the world of the dead. Charon, the ferryman, a grumpy old man with a terrible temper, rowed the soul across in return for a small fee. This is why corpses were buried with a coin in their mouths. They also took honey cakes to feed to Cerberus, a terrible three-headed watchdog. Cerberus guarded the gate to the Underworld and ate anyone who tried to escape!

HEAVEN AND HELL

NEXT, it was believed the soul came to a crossroads. Here three judges decided its fate, based on its past deeds. Virtuous people who had led good lives were sent to the heavenly Elysian Fields, a beautiful place of peace and happiness, filled with golden sunshine. Wicked or cruel souls were sent to Tartarus, a hellish place of torment and punishment (see p.136). People who had been neither very good nor bad were sent to the Asphodel Fields, a rather boring sort of place.

ISLES OF THE BLESSED

SOME Greeks believed in another Heaven or paradise, called the Isles of the Blessed. The islands lay somewhere far across the sea, to the west, and were ruled by the giant Cronos. They were said to be covered with cornfields, meadows, and rose gardens and swept by warm ocean breezes. In the fields, the corn grew ripe by itself and honey dripped from the trees. The weather was always warm and spring-like, with no storms, rain, or winter. These were lands where time stood still. No one grew old, and there was no work to do. The islanders spent their time playing games, riding, and playing the lyre. Their lives were blessed indeed.

This is the place where the road divides and leads in two directions. One way is to the right and extends under the ramparts of Dis (Pluto) to Elysium. But the left path leads to the evil realms of Tartarus where the penalties for sin are exacted.

Virgil
Aeneid

SAFE ARRIVAL

FOR the Greeks and Romans, a proper funeral was very important. Without the correct rituals, they believed that souls wandered for ever, lost and alone, along the banks of the River Styx, unable to enter the Underworld. After being carefully washed and dressed, the body was taken to the cemetery. Rich people were buried in elaborate tombs. Some even had their own kitchens and dining rooms where the dead person's family came for a meal on the anniversary of their death.

The last day does not bring extinction, but a change of place.

Cicero

THE BLESSED
OTHERWORLD

THE Celts lived in Britain and north-western Europe from about 3000 BCE They told many stories about the Otherworld, a group of islands over the sea to the far west, where the souls of the dead lived side by side with the gods and fairies. They believed that, when you died, your soul was reborn in the Otherworld. Usually, the Otherworld was hidden by a magic mist. But, on one night of the year, it could be seen by the living. This was the Feast of Samhain, on 1 November, when the gates of the Otherworld were opened and the souls of the dead roamed the Earth, taking revenge on those who had wronged them.

THE OTHERWORLD

IN the Otherworld lay Tir na n'Oc, the Land of the Young or the Shimmering Land, which was the Celtic Heaven. It was a land of eternal youth and happiness, where the magic cauldron of the great god, Dagha, provided a never-ending feast of food and drink. Here the souls of the dead were lulled to sleep by the songs of beautiful birds. There was no fighting, illness, or old age. Whatever your soul desired, it received. The king of the Otherworld was Manannan, god of sea, magic and rebirth.

BLESSED ISLES

THE story of King Arthur and his Knights of the Round Table probably came from the Celts. Arthur was an English king, famous for his courage and good deeds. Legend says, that when he died in battle, three fairy women came with a boat to take him to the paradise of Avalon, the magical island of apples. It was ruled over by Morgan, the fairy queen. Some people believe that Avalon still exists on Earth, in Glastonbury, Somerset, in south-west England.

THE VOYAGE OF BRAN

CELTIC legends tell of the time when sometimes people from the land of the living visited the Otherworld. One of these was the great hero, Bran. One night, a woman appeared in his dreams, bearing a branch of a tree from the Otherworld. Sent by Manannan, she urged Bran to visit this magical place. With 26 companions, Bran set sail. First he crossed the Delightful Plain, then came to the Land Under Waves, where he met the great Manannan himself. Next, he traveled to the Island of Merriment, where people did nothing but laugh with joy.

Soon one of the voyagers, Nechtan, became homesick. The queen of the island allowed them to leave but gave them this warning: "Whatever you do, do not set foot on land," she said. Nechtan ignored her words. When they reached Ireland, he leapt ashore, and immediately turned to ashes. For although only a year had passed in the Otherworld, many centuries had passed on Earth. And when Bran told the waiting people his name, they did not know him, but had heard his story in their ancient legends, so much time had passed. Then Bran sailed away from there, never to be seen again.

This story is sometimes understood as the story of the journey of the soul as it passes from life to death.

SPIRIT LANDSCAPES

In the traditional beliefs of Africa and Australia, nature is alive with spirits. They are believed to live in trees, in birds and animals, and in the features of the landscape. They are worshiped by people who live close to nature and rely on nature for their survival and food. Through their actions, good or bad, the spirits control what happens to them in this world and beyond.

RETURN TO THE DREAMING

The Aborigines of Australia believe that the world was made long ago, in a time called the Dreaming. Then the spirits of the ancestors roamed the land, some as humans, some as animals, giving the landscape its shape. The Aborigines believe that the land is sacred. It is part of them, as they are part of it. When you die, they believe, your soul returns to the Dreaming. It does not go to another place far away, but remains part of the sacred land.

FUNERAL DANCE

At an Aborigine funeral, there are many ceremonies to speed the soul home. Songs are sung, then the coffin is painted with mystical symbols to guide the soul on its journey. Then the dancing begins. The dancers paint themselves with yellow clay, and stamp their feet and sticks on the ground, to drive away evil spirits. Then the coffin is buried in the ground. Some time later, the bones are removed, washed, and placed in a cave or near a waterhole, to continue their journey to their heavenly home.

LANDS OF THE DEAD

In many parts of Africa, people traditionally believe that when you die, your soul travels to the land of the dead. This may be up in the sky, reached by a rope or spider's web, or under the ground, reached through a cave or a burrow. But many souls also wander the Earth as ghosts. Some have a message to bring to the living. Some want justice or revenge. Others keep watch over loved ones, helping with their worries or needs. A wise person keeps on the right side of the spirits. If the spirits are angry, who knows what mayhem and mischief they may cause.

HOW DEATH CAME TO THE WORLD

THIS African story tells how one day, when the world was new, God sent for Chameleon and gave him this message to take to Earth: "People will not die. When their time on Earth is finished, they will go away, then return from time to time like the Moon."

Chameleon learned the message by heart and set off on his way. But he walked so slowly, as chameleons do, and stopped so often to eat and rest, that it took him days and days to reach the Earth. God began to worry. What could have happened to Chameleon? Had he lost his way? He was usually so careful and reliable.

God decided to send another messenger, just in case. He called for Hare, one of the fastest, cleverest of all animals, and gave him the same message to take to Earth. In great excitement, Hare mumbled the message back, then sped off. In no time at all, he reached Earth. He raced into the people's village ... and tried to remember what God's message had said.

"Now, what was it?" he said. "Ah, yes ... People will die," he told the villagers. "When their time on Earth is finished, they will go away and not return."

Then he raced back to God. Shortly afterwards, Chameleon arrived. But it was too late. And this is how death came to the world. All because the hasty Hare made a mistake.

TOWARDS THE GREAT SPIRIT

AMONG the Native Americans, life and death are closely linked. Most people believe in a Great Spirit who created the Earth and is thought to live in the sky. Every living thing in nature also has a spirit. Many Native Americans believe that death is nothing to be frightened of. It is a journey you will have prepared for throughout your earthly life. Then your soul will soar up to the Great Spirit, who first created it, and take its place in the spirit world. When you die, you simply move from one world to another, passing from a world of darkness to a land of light.

HAPPY HUNTING GROUND

IN the old days, many Native Americans lived by hunting and fishing. So important were animals in their lives that they pictured the next world as the "happy hunting grounds" where the plains were always full of buffalo, and the rivers full of fish. Here the souls of people who had died spent the day hunting and the night feasting and dancing around campfires lit by their ancestors. You can see these campfires from Earth, as the stars in the night sky.

THE THUNDERBIRD

WHILE the Great Spirit rules over all creation, the everyday running of the Universe is left to powerful spirits of nature. Among many Native Americans the greatest of these is the mighty Thunderbird. This enormous eagle is the spirit of thunder. Its beating wings make the sound of thunder. Its eyes and beak flash lightning. It is strong enough to carry off whales. Terrifying though it is, the Thunderbird is also a welcome spirit. For it brings rain to keep the Earth from drying up and the crops from dying. The Thunderbird is constantly battling the spirits of evil. Their clashes cause earthquakes, floods, and storms. Anyone struck by lightning was thought very lucky. They were said to possess some of the Thunderbird's magical powers.

A little while and I will be gone from among you, whither I cannot tell. From nowhere we come, into nowhere we go. What is life? It is the flash of a firefly in the night. It is the breath of a buffalo in the winter time. It is as the little shadow that runs across the grass and loses itself in the sunset.

Chief Crowfoot of the Blackfoot

THE SPIRIT ROAD

THIS is how the Native Americans of the Thompson River in Canada pictured the journey to the next world.

The country of the souls is beneath us, away towards the sunset. On the trail, you can see the tracks of those who have gone before you, and their dogs. The trail is long and winding and painted with red clay. After a while, it reaches a wide, shallow stream of crystal clear water. Across it lies a long, slender log on which the tracks of the souls can be seen. When you cross the log, you find yourself on the trail again. This time it climbs, higher and higher, to the top of a high hill. The hill is littered with belongings which the souls have brought from the land of the living and must now leave here. From there, the trail is wide and level. Three guardians, old, gray-haired, and wise, sit by the roadside to send back those souls whose time is not yet come. At the end of the trail, there is a great lodge. Here the friends and relatives who have gone before you, meet and wait for your soul. As you approach, they call out your name to welcome you. Inside the lodge, it is warm and light, with a sweet smell of flowers and fresh grass. The people dance and sing, and beat their drums. They lift you on to their shoulders, so happy are they to see you again.

When it is your time to pass, it should be with your mind wide open and your prayer in your heart. When one dear to you dies, do not be sad at your loss. Feel happy that now their soul is free to soar to the Great Spirit, our common Creator. Where there is love, there is no room to fear.

Sun Bear

Heavenly Bodies

IF you stand outside on a dark night and look up at the sky, what do you see? The waxy face of the man in the Moon? The twinkling stars? The darkness of space, stretching as far as the eye can see? From ancient times, people have held the skies in awe. Before they understood the science of the stars, the skies seemed a vast, mysterious place, a suitable place for the gods to live. Today, we still sometimes use the word "Heaven" to mean the skies. But we know much more about them. Modern telescopes, satellites, and gigantic space rockets have shown us more than ever before. But the skies continue to amaze and fascinate us. And space exploration is full of magical moments. Can you imagine how it must have felt to be the first person to step on to the moon? It must have seemed like Heaven indeed.

EARLY ASTRONOMERS

As long as people have lived on Earth, they have gazed at the skies in wonder and tried to understand what they saw. Not only did early people worship the heavenly bodies as gods, they also used them to tell the time and find the way. Many people believed that their very lives and destinies were controlled by the sun, moon, and stars. They consulted astronomers to find out the future. These star-gazers often had a dual role as priests and they were powerful people within the community. Today modern astronomers continue to search for hidden galaxies and other futures on planets whose destinies may be linked to ours.

CLOCKS AND CALENDARS

TODAY it is easy to find out the time or check a date on the calendar. Early people had no such ways of telling the time. Instead they used the sun, moon, and stars as their clocks. The day began when the sun rose and ended when it set. The phases of the moon marked the passing months. The earliest calendars were devised by astronomers to fix the dates for religious festivals. They too were based on the movements of the heavenly bodies.

STONEHENGE

ANCIENT stone circles are found all over the world. But why they were built is still a mystery. One of the most famous circles is Stonehenge in southern England. Dating from about 3,000 BCE, Stonehenge was for a long time thought to have been built as an ancient temple to the sun. But some modern scientists have another theory. They suggest that the stones were a giant calendar used by early astronomers to plot the position of the sun and stars, and to calculate the length of the year.

"In Heaven, people live on a sort of shooting star. It is gold and silver and all the colors. You see God when you get to Heaven. He is a young man standing on the shooting star."

Bill Cunningham
aged 5

This clock was made about 1390. The moon is in the center surrounded by stars. The hour hand is a gold sun.

AMAZING DISCOVERIES

ASTRONOMY is one of the oldest sciences, practiced for thousands of years. Until the invention of the telescope in the seventeenth century, though, astronomers could only study what they could see with their own eyes. Even so, they made some amazing discoveries. A Greek, Hipparchus, counted 850 stars, long before anyone else. Anaxagoras realized that the moon did not shine with its own light but reflected the light of the sun. Sometimes things went badly wrong. Another Greek, Heraclitus, calculated that the sun was just 1ft (30 centimeters) across. The true figure is a staggering 868,000 miles (1.4 *million* kilometers)!

EARTH IN SPACE

FOR hundreds of years, scientists believed that the Earth lay at the center of the Universe, and that the sun, moon, and planets revolved around it. It was not until the seventeenth century that they were proved wrong. Using the newly-invented telescope, Italian astronomer, Galileo Galilei, made a startling discovery – that the Earth and the planets actually rotate round the sun. Galileo's views brought him into bitter conflict with the teachings of the Catholic Church which stated that God had created the Universe with the Earth in the center. Galileo was put on trial and forced to renounce his discoveries. He was only officially pardoned in 1992!

If the north wind sweeps the face of Heaven until the appearance of the new Moon, the harvest will be abundant.

Babylonian divination tablet

EYES ON THE SKIES

MODERN **astronomers have very sophisticated equipment to help them look far into outer space. Telescopes and planetary probes have detected objects near and far away, and space travel has revolutionized our knowledge of the skies. So has science left any room for Heaven? Does each new piece of knowledge mean that a little bit more of Heaven is lost? Or is there room for both science and spiritual beliefs? Some people believe that the more scientists discover about the Universe the more we can marvel at God's creation of the world.**

THE BIG BANG

IN the past, people used creation stories to explain how the world began (see pages 60, 61). But most modern astronomers believe that the Universe began 15,000 million years ago, with a gigantic explosion called the Big Bang. An Unimaginably Enormous Bang! This scattered energy and tiny bits of matter out into space where they created the galaxies and other heavenly bodies. The Earth formed about 4,500 million years ago. Recent studies show that the Universe is still expanding with the force of the Big Bang, as the outermost galaxies rush further out into space.

THE UNIVERSE

THE Universe is everything that you see in the night sky . . . and more besides. Our own part of the Universe is called the solar system. It includes the Earth and eight other planets which orbit the sun (these are Mercury, Venus, Mars, Jupiter, Saturn, Uranus, Neptune, and Pluto). Many of the planets, including the Earth, have moons travelling around them. To us, the sun is very special indeed. Without its heat and light, nothing could live on Earth. But it is just one of billions of stars in the Universe. And some of these may also have planets spinning around them.

MAN ON THE MOON

ON July 20 1969, American astronaut Neil Armstrong got closer to Heaven than most of us could ever dream of. Watched by millions of television viewers all over the world, he became the first person to set foot on the moon. "That's one small step for a man," he said, "one giant leap for mankind." Armstrong and fellow astronaut Buzz Aldrin spent two and a half hours on the moon, conducting experiments and collecting samples of moon rock. A little bit of the mystery of Heaven had been won, or lost.

STARDUST

A STRONOMERS continue to search the skies and make extraordinary discoveries. And there is plenty more left to learn. In February 1999, NASA (the National Aeronautical and Space Administration) launched the spacecraft *Stardust* on a seven-year journey to the stars. In the year 2004, *Stardust* will pass by Comet Wild-2, closer than a spacecraft has ever come before. Its mission is to trap some dust from the comet, believed to be from the Big Bang itself. It is set to return to Earth in 2006. So, keep watching . . .

"We sent up Yuri Gagarin to see if he could find the kingdom of Heaven, and he couldn't find it. He circled the Earth and found nothing in outer space – just complete darkness . . . nothing that looked like paradise. So we sent up Herman Titov to take another look, in case Gagarin had missed it. And he couldn't find it either."

Kruschev, leader of the Communist Party in the former Soviet Union, on the first manned spaceflight in 1961

IS THERE ANYBODY OUT THERE?

> *"The creature was about 90 cm tall, with very thin arms and legs. Its face was pale like wax. I didn't notice the eyes, but the nose was very strange. It was a hook rather than a nose. The ears were very small and narrow towards the head. The creature wore some sort of overall in a light green material. On its feet were boots of a darker green color."*
>
> **Aarno Heinonen, Finland, January 1970**

As far as we know, our Earth is the only planet in the Universe known to be able to support life. But there's really no reason to suppose that we are all alone in space. There may be many other solar systems, with planets traveling around their own suns. There may be other creatures and civilizations living on these planets, busily inventing their own spacecraft, and trying to reach other worlds. Who knows, there may even be alien spacecraft speeding towards us at this very moment. Imagine if one landed near you. What would you say if you met a real-life ET, or extraterrestrial? Perhaps you already know one?

FLYING SAUCERS

MANY people claim to have seen UFOs (Unidentified Flying Objects) in the sky. Some UFOs have even been photographed. One of the most famous sightings was made by American pilot Kenneth Arnold as he flew over Mount Rainier, USA, in 1947. He saw a flash of light and nine objects which moved "like a saucer would if you skipped it across the water." The term "flying saucer" was born! Since then, there have been millions of UFO sightings, many of them very similar. But are these really vehicles from outer space or simply ordinary aircraft, tricks of the light, unusual weather, or even deliberate fakes? Nobody can be certain. Some people believe that these alien visitors were the "gods" of ancient mythologies.

CLOSE ENCOUNTERS

HAVE extraterrestrials already landed on Earth? Some people certainly think so. They claim to have been abducted, or kidnapped, by aliens. In 1961, Betty and Barney Hill were driving home through the White Mountains in New Hampshire. Suddenly a bright object appeared from the sky and hovered above the ground. They could just make out the shapes of several figures inside. But the next few hours were a total blank. The Hills could not remember what had happened or how they eventually reached home. Later, under hypnosis, they told their dramatic story, claiming that they had been taken from their car by a group of gray-skinned aliens and examined on board their spaceship.

And I looked, and, behold, a whirlwind came out of the north, a great cloud, and and fire infolding itself, and a brightness was about it, and out of the midst thereof as the color of amber, out of the midst of the fire.

Ezekiel, Chapter 1: verse 4

SCI-FI FRIGHT

EXTRATERRESTRIALS, future worlds and travel to outer space have captured the imagination of many science-fiction writers and film-makers. Sci-fi mixes science with make-believe, all too realistically sometimes! In 1938, H. G. Wells's famous sci-fi novel, *War of the Worlds*, was adapted for radio. It told of an alien invasion from Mars, set in New York. It was so convincing that many listeners believed that a Martian invasion had really taken place. Terrible panic followed.

CALLING ALL ALIENS!

OPERATION SETI (Search for Extraterrestrial Intelligence) was set up in 1982 to try to make contact with aliens, rather than waiting for the aliens to make the first move. It has several radio telescopes around the world which blast signals deep into space. Sadly, there have been no replies so far. Other attempts to communicate with aliens include the long-playing records carried by the *Voyager* 1 and 2 planetary probes. The records are called "Sounds of the Earth" and feature music and greetings in 60 languages, together with bird and whale songs.

STARS OF THE FUTURE

Do you ever read your horoscope in the newspaper or a magazine? People called astrologers work out these forecasts for the future from the position of the stars in each sign of the zodiac. It can be fun to see if what they say comes true. Astrology is the name given to the practice of telling the future from the stars. It has been in use since ancient times. Most importantly, it fixed our births and lives as part of a grand cosmic plan, determined by the forces of Heaven. At first, it was closely linked to astronomy but now the two are often quite separate.

HINDU HOROSCOPES

WHEN a Hindu baby is born, the priest casts its horoscope, based on the position of the stars and planets at the exact minute of its birth. From this, he reads the baby's future and suggests a suitable name. Horoscopes are also used in later life to fix favorable, times and dates for weddings and other celebrations.

Silently, one by one,
In the infinite meadows of heaven,
Blossomed the lovely stars.
The forget-me-nots of the angels.
Henry Wadsworth Longfellow

SIGNS OF THE ZODIAC

IF you know your birth sign, you already know something about astrology. The Zodiac is made up of twelve "sun signs", each related to a constellation, a pattern of stars in the sky. Some constellations make the shape of animals or people: for example, Taurus the bull, or Sagittarius, the archer. They were first identified by the ancient Sumerians 5,000 years ago and later adapted by the Greeks. Even today, some people believe that their lives and personalities are strongly affected by their sun signs. For example, people born under the sign of Pisces are said to be dreamy and sensitive. What sign of the Zodiac are you?

Aries, the ram	*March 21 – April 20*
Taurus, the bull	*April 21 – May 21*
Gemini, the twins	*May 22 – June 21*
Cancer, the crab	*June 22 – July 22*
Leo, the lion	*July 23 – August 23*
Virgo, the maiden	*August 24 – September 22*
Libra, the scales	*September 23 – October 23*
Scorpio, the scorpion	*October 24 – November 22*
Sagittarius, the archer	*November 23 – December 21*
Capricorn, the goat	*December 22 – January 20*
Aquarius, the water carrier	*January 21 – February 18*
Pisces, the fish	*February 19 – March 20*

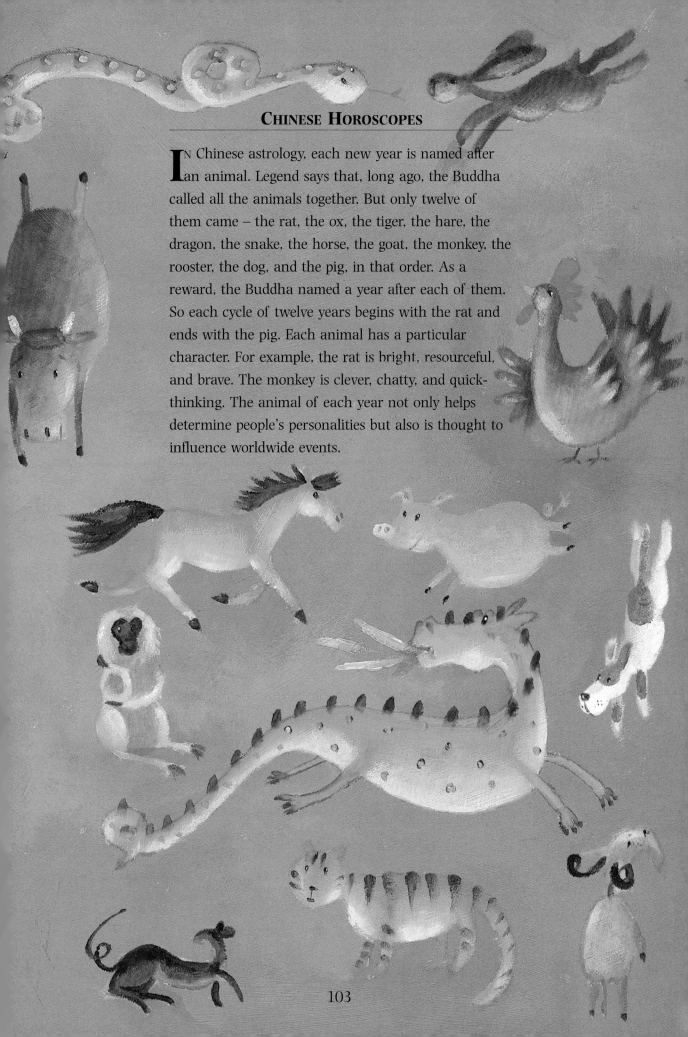

CHINESE HOROSCOPES

In Chinese astrology, each new year is named after an animal. Legend says that, long ago, the Buddha called all the animals together. But only twelve of them came – the rat, the ox, the tiger, the hare, the dragon, the snake, the horse, the goat, the monkey, the rooster, the dog, and the pig, in that order. As a reward, the Buddha named a year after each of them. So each cycle of twelve years begins with the rat and ends with the pig. Each animal has a particular character. For example, the rat is bright, resourceful, and brave. The monkey is clever, chatty, and quick-thinking. The animal of each year not only helps determine people's personalities but also is thought to influence worldwide events.

Heaven on Earth

IF you do not have religious beliefs, can you get to Heaven too? Some people think that, by making this world a better place to live in, we can create Heaven on Earth. This might mean trying to live a good life, and caring for the environment, animals, and other people. Other people think that Heaven is having money and possessions, or living lives free from work, stress, and strain. But are they right? Or do all these things give only a brief glimpse of Heaven which is quickly gone? Is Heaven on Earth a place deep inside you, or simply the feeling of being happy or at peace with yourself? Is Heaven on Earth what you make it?

HEAVEN ON EARTH

MANY people believe that, by living a good life, you can find the joy and happiness of Heaven here on Earth. By trying to make this world a better place, you can help create Heaven for yourself and others. This might mean making the most of yourself and your own life, or doing someone else a good turn. It might mean being fit and healthy, making friends, or falling in love. It's really up to you.

WORLD PEACE

SOME people think that Heaven on Earth would be a world without war, famine, or poverty. Wars may be caused by politics, religion, or other differences of opinions. But it is often innocent people who get caught in the crossfire and suffer most. And fighting is not the only problem. War also destroys people's homes and livelihoods. When you see pictures of refugees or starving people on the news, it can be difficult to watch. But, ideally, they also make you think about people less fortunate than yourself and about how you could help them.

AID WORKERS

ALL over the world, aid organizations try to help people in trouble. Many of the workers are volunteers who sometimes risk their own lives to help others. They work in places hit by natural disasters, such as hurricanes or earthquakes, and in war zones or refugee camps. They help to provide food, water, shelter, and medical care, often under difficult and dangerous circumstances. For them, Heaven is making a difference, even if it can only be a small one.

POLITICS AND HEAVEN

SOME people have used politics to try to create Heaven on Earth. According to the nineteeth century German philosopher, Karl Marx, the ideal world was one in which everyone was equal, with the same opportunities for all, not just for the privileged few. Marx believed that social justice, rather than religion, was the only way to Heaven. Communist Russia followed Marx's ideas but never really achieved the sort of Heaven for its people that Marx had hoped for.

"My idea of Heaven is a place where there is no poverty, where people don't get any illnesses, where nobody is fighting, killing and maiming anybody else.
It would be a place where everybody could live in peace and harmony."

Julekha Khan
computer trainer

DREAMING OF HEAVEN

THE American preacher and leader Martin Luther King spent his life fighting for equal rights for black people. In the 1960s, in the USA, black people were often treated very unfairly because of the color of their skin. Martin Luther King wanted everyone to be treated the same. "I have a dream," he told his supporters in a famous speech, "that my four little children will one day live in a nation where they will not be judged, by the color of their skin, but by the content of their character . . ." This was his dream of Heaven. What is yours?

Martin Luther King (1929 – 1968) risked his life to end racial prejudice in the USA. He was murdered in 1968, aged just 39.

HEAVENLY GARDENS

IN many beliefs, Heaven is pictured as a beautiful garden. And some people use their love of nature to transform their own gardens into Heaven on Earth. Do you like gardening? What would you plant in a heavenly garden? To create a place full of sweetness and light, you could use plants with soft colors, such as cream, mauve, or pink. For a feeling of calm, add some sweet-smelling herbs. And don't forget to leave plenty of places for birds and wild animals to shelter. Looking after the world's ecology responsibly is a way of ensuring a Heaven on Earth rather than the opposite.

ANIMAL HEAVENS

Do you have a pet? Perhaps you have a cat or dog, or a hamster, or a goldfish? Does your pet have a name? Millions of us have household pets. They keep us company and cheer us up when we're feeling down. We like playing with them and talking to them. And they don't answer back! When a pet dies, it can be a very sad and upsetting time. It can take a long time to feel better again. But feeling sad is perfectly normal. After all, our pets are part of the family too.

PETS IN HEAVEN

Do you think that pets go to Heaven? And if so, what is their Heaven like? For cats, Heaven is probably a place full of fish to eat, mice to chase, balls of string to play with, and cosy chairs to snuggle down in. For dogs, it may be an endless supply of juicy bones, slippers to chew, long muddy walks, and lots and lots of neighborhood cats to chase! As for pet Heaven on Earth, what better than a caring home, kindness, and lots of love and attention. And that's where you come in.

> *Not to hurt our humble brethren is our first duty to them, but to stop there is not enough. We have a higher mission – to be of service to them wherever they require it.*
>
> **St. Francis of Assisi**

ELEPHANT HEAVEN

WE often think that being sad when a loved one dies is something that only human beings feel. But some wild animals show grief too. Elephants live in very tightly-knit families. When an elephant dies, the other members of its group gather around its body, keeping very quiet and still. Then they touch and stroke the body, as if they are saying goodbye. They do the same if they come across the bones of an elephant which has died.

CARING FOR ANIMALS

WORLDWIDE, many people are working hard to stop animals being badly treated. They believe that, like people, animals deserve to be treated with kindness and respect, whether they are on farms, in zoos, or on the racetrack. Many wild animals are also in danger from hunting or because their homes are being destroyed. There are many groups involved in trying to save them. Perhaps you belong to one yourself?

ANIMAL RITES

IN his book, *Animal Rites*, Professor Andrew Linzey sets out special words and prayers to celebrate the life of animals, to say thank you for their companionship, and to mark a pet's death. These services are written to be used in a Christian church but non-Christians may also find their words helpful. And you can always write your own celebration of your pet. This is part of a prayer for a pet's burial.

Holy Creator
give us eyes to see
and ears to hear
how every living thing
speaks to us of your love.

Even in our sorrow
we have cause for joy
for we know that
this creature
who died on Earth
shall live again in Heaven.

FALSE HEAVENS

SOME **people think that they have found Heaven on Earth but their Heaven turns out to be false. They think they know what will make them happy. This might be having lots of money or a big house, or using drugs and alcohol. But they quickly find that this sort of happiness doesn't last very long, and is very quickly over. It doesn't take their worries or problems away. True Heaven needs to be something more, something that comes from inside you.**

TOO MUCH MONEY?

HAVE you ever wished that you had more money to buy all the things you want? Many people think that having lots of money would be Heaven on Earth. But does being rich make you happy? People who have won a lottery, for example, often find that it changes their lives for the worse. It seems that happiness is not something you can buy, however much money you have. Money can cause problems at other times too. Think about Christmas. It is so much about spending money on presents, cards, and food that its real meaning, to celebrate the birth of Jesus Christ, is often lost.

TAKING DRUGS

A drug is a chemical which affects your body. If you are ill, the doctor might give you some medicine, a type of drug, to make you better. But some people take drugs for fun to change their moods. They say these drugs make them feel better or happier. But these feelings aren't based on real life happiness. They are false and do not last. And the drugs themselves are very dangerous. Many young people have died from taking drugs. Others have had their lives ruined. They become so dependent on them that they cannot live without them. Then they are said to be addicted. Learning to do without drugs can be hard. It is much better never to take them.

FAT AND THIN

In Western society, being slim like the models you see in magazines or on the television is often seen as meaning being happy and attractive. It is not very fashionable to be fat. But is this another false Heaven? It is true that being very overweight can be bad for your health but being too thin can be just as unhealthy. Some people try to make themselves slim by eating too little but this can make them ill and unhappy instead. The most important thing is to feel happy with who you are and not worry about what you *think* you should be like.

SIMPLE LIVES

Some people, such as Christian monks and nuns, or Hindu holy men, choose to give up their homes, possessions, and other luxuries, and live very simply instead. They leave their families and dedicate their lives to God. Their faith or beliefs give their lives focus and meaning. Many religions teach that wanting money and possessions is what makes people unhappy. Being contented with your life and lot is what makes a true Heaven on Earth.

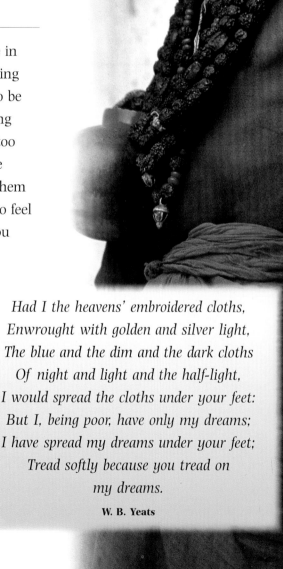

Had I the heavens' embroidered cloths,
Enwrought with golden and silver light,
The blue and the dim and the dark cloths
Of night and light and the half-light,
I would spread the cloths under your feet:
But I, being poor, have only my dreams;
I have spread my dreams under your feet;
Tread softly because you tread on
my dreams.

W. B. Yeats

A Hindu holy man, or sadhu.

CHILDREN'S HEAVENS

AND now it's your turn! What is your own idea of Heaven on Earth? It might be something that you have spent ages wishing for or waiting for, like going on holiday to a favorite place or looking forward to your birthday. Or it might be a special person, or a treasured possession which makes you feel particularly happy. It might be sharing your things with someone else, or being kind to a friend in trouble. It can be as serious or funny as you like. It can even be sad – it's really up to you. You'll have to use your imagination.

"I think that Heaven is another dimension which you enter once you die. It is just made up of very powerful energy which allows you to have whatever you want, to do whatever you want, and to know whatever you want. To me Heaven would be exploring the galaxy in a starship."

Thomas King
aged 11

The gates of Heaven are so easily found when we are little, and they are always standing open to let children wander in.

J.M. Barrie
Sentimental Journey

Visions of Heaven

HAVE you ever thought that something was so interesting that it inspired you to write a poem about it or draw a picture of it? For centuries, the idea of Heaven has inspired artists, composers, writers, and builders to create their greatest and most lasting works. Not only do they sing God's praises they also help touch us with a little piece of Heaven. They are a helpful way of voicing beliefs and capturing moods of joy, hope, or sorrow which can otherwise be difficult to express. Have you ever heard a piece of music or seen a picture that has moved you to tears or made your spine tingle? The Arts can have the power to lift your spirits from the everyday and send them soaring.

HEAVENLY MUSIC

SOME people say that you'll have to wait for Heaven to hear the most beautiful music of all, sung by the angels. But here on Earth, Heaven has inspired some of the most glorious and uplifting music ever, from classical to pop, hymns, prayers, and spirituals. Music plays a very important part in many religions. Singing and playing musical instruments not only allows worshipers to express their feelings but also are a tuneful way of sending their hopes and prayers up to Heaven.

HEAVENLY VOICES

"The heavens are telling the glory of God, The wonder of his work displays the firmament."

THIS is a famous chorus from a work called the *Creation* by the German composer, Franz Joseph Haydn. It tells the story of the creation of the world from the Book of Genesis in the Bible. In Western Europe many classical composers set their music to passages from the Bible or other sacred texts. In the *Creation*, the words are sung by four soloists who play the parts of the angels Raphael, Uriel, and Gabriel, accompanied by a choir. Have a listen, if you can.

TEMPLE MUSIC

INDIAN classical music is not written down. Musicians learn patterns of notes called ragas and improvise, or make up, the music around them. There are hundreds of different ragas, for different times of the day. Each is designed to set a mood, such as love, courage, sorrow, or worship. Playing a raga is said to be like building a temple. First, you have to lay the foundations, then you build the walls and roof, and then you add the decorations. Finally you bring God into the temple.

KNOCKIN' ON HEAVEN'S DOOR

Bob Dylan

*Momma take this badge off 'a me
I can't use it anymore
It's gettin' dark, too dark to see
Feel I'm knockin' on heaven's door*

*Knock-knock-knockin' on heaven's door
Knock-knock-knockin' on heaven's door
Knock-knock-knockin' on heaven's door
Knock-knock-knockin' on heaven's door.*

*Momma put my guns on the ground
I can't shoot them anymore
The long, black cloud is comin' down
I feel I'm knockin' on heaven's door.*

MUSIC IN HELL

THE "other place," Hell, has inspired some great music too. In an opera by Mozart, a nobleman called Don Giovanni is in love with Donna Anna but his feelings are not returned. He kills her strict father, the Commendatore (commander). Anna and her fiancé swear to take revenge but Giovanni manages to escape. Hiding in the graveyard, he hears the voice of the Commendatore's statue speaking to him. It orders him to ask forgiveness for his sins. When Giovanni refuses, the statue drags him down into the flames of Hell. The story has a strong moral to teach , that wicked people always get their just deserts.

HEAVENLY FILMS

MANY films have been inspired by the idea of Heaven. In the 1946 film *It's a Wonderful Life*, starring James Stewart, an angel comes down to Earth at Christmas to save a man from taking his own life. Thanks to the angel, the film ends happily ever after. The film was one of many movies made in Hollywood after World War II to lift people's spirits and to make them feel more optimistic about the future. More recent films like *Michael*, with John Travolta, *Meet Joe Black*, and T.V. series like *Teen Angel* have all shown that people still believe in heavenly intervention.

"I shall hear in Heaven."
The last words of deaf composer, Ludwig van Beethoven

11

HEAVEN IN WORDS

MILLIONS of books, stories, and poems have been written about Heaven. Maybe you've read some of them? Perhaps they've inspired you to write some heavenly words of your own? Heaven has fascinated writers for centuries. This may be because putting our deepest feelings into words often helps us to understand them better.

DIVINE COMEDY

THE *Divine Comedy* was written by the Italian poet Dante in the early fourteenth century. The poem tells the story of Dante's journey through Hell to Heaven, and to the "love that moves the sun and all the stars." Dante describes Heaven and Hell as made up of nine circles. Your soul goes to a different circle, depending how saintly or sinful you are. Certain circles were reserved for people who were mean, greedy, or bad-tempered. Dante's pictures of Heaven and Hell were so vivid that some people at the time thought he had really been there.

EVERYONE SANG

by Siegfried Sassoon

Everyone suddenly burst out singing;
And I was filled with such delight
As prisoned birds must find in freedom,
Winging wildly across the white
Orchards and dark-green fields; on – on –
and out of sight.

Everyone's voice was suddenly lifted;
And beauty came like the setting sun;
My heart was shaken with tears; and horror
Drifted away . . . O, but Everyone
Was a bird; and the song was wordless; the
singing will never be done.

IN HEAVEN

by Caitlin Wynne, aged 9

When you arrive in holy
Heaven
The holy gates open.
Spirits of people welcome
you.
The voice of angels
You can hear.
Clouds fly past
All day long.
Spirits stand on clouds
and silently whisper.
Heaven is a wonderful
place to be.

GUIDE TO HEAVEN

THE *Tibetan Book of the Dead* is an ancient guide to Heaven, written about 1200 years ago. It is read aloud at Buddhist funerals to help the dead person's soul on its journey to its next rebirth. The book describes the worlds through which the soul will pass – the realms of the gods, giants, people, ghosts, and Hell. Each is shown by a different-colored light. If you find yourself drawn towards a particular light, you will be reborn in that realm.

THE SELFISH GIANT

by Oscar Wilde

Every day, the children played in the giant's garden. It was a beautiful garden, with soft green grass, sweet-smelling flowers and twelve huge peach trees.

One day the giant came home, after seven long years away. When he saw the children, he shooed them away. Then he built a high wall around his garden. He was a very selfish giant.

Spring came. Everywhere, birds sang and trees burst into leaf. But in the giant's garden, it was still winter. Every day, the giant looked outside, wondering when the sun would shine.

Then, one day, he heard the sound of a bird singing outside his window! And he saw an extraordinary sight. His garden was full of children. And the garden was so happy to see them that it had burst into life. Only in one corner was it still winter. A little boy stood there, too small to climb the tree. The giant crept downstairs and out into the garden. But when the children saw him, they ran away and Winter came back again. Only the little boy was left. Gently, the giant lifted him into the tree which at once burst into bloom. From then on, the giant played with the children every day. But he never saw the little boy again.

The years passed and the giant grew old and gray. One winter morning, he saw a wonderful sight. In the far corner of the garden was a tree covered in lovely blossom, with golden branches and silver fruit. And underneath stood the little boy. The giant rushed outside. On the boy's hands he saw the marks of two nails, with another two on his feet. Then the giant was filled with wonder. He knew that this was Jesus and the giant knelt down in front of him.

"You let me play in your garden once," the little boy said with a smile, "now I will take you to my garden in Paradise."

And when the children came to play that afternoon, they found the giant lying dead under the tree, covered all over in blossom.

HEAVENLY ART

FROM the earliest times, people have used art to express their deepest hopes and fears. Paintings were found in the caves of prehistoric people. Thousands of years ago, they painted pictures of bulls, bison, deer, and mammoths. Painting these animals had a special purpose. It is thought that the artists believed they would bring good luck in the hunt. Since then, art has been used to express not only what happens in real life but also what people think might happen, including their vision of Heaven.

A painting by Stanley Spencer showing the Resurrection in a modern setting. You can see the dead people emerging from the paving stones and greeting each other.

PAINTINGS OF HEAVEN

THE idea of Heaven and what it might be like has inspired some of the world's greatest artists. But these were more than works of art. Years ago, pictures of Heaven were used to encourage worshipers to live good lives. Pictures of Hell were used as warnings!

WINDOWS TO GOD

PAINTINGS called icons are very important in the Orthodox Church. They often show portraits of Jesus or the saints and are used as a focus for worship. People light candles and incense in front of them, and say their prayers. But icons are much more than simply pictures. They are believed to bring the worshiper into the real presence of the figure shown, like windows into Heaven.

SACRED CIRCLE

A mandala is a circular painting used by some Buddhists to meditate. It is like a map or guide for a person's spiritual progress. Working from the outside in, they pass first through three circles of purity, rebirth, and enlightenment until they reach four gateways. These lead them to a central object or figure which symbolizes a quality such as compassion or wisdom. The figure may be the Buddha or another heavenly being. Colors are also important. They stand for different heavens or different qualities.

"God is really only another artist. He invented the elephant, the giraffe, and the cat. He has no real style. He just goes on trying other things."

Pablo Picasso

A mandala.

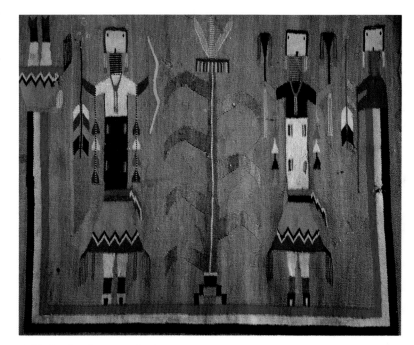

A blanket based on a sand painting.

PAINTING IN SAND

AMONG the Navaho people of the USA, sacred sandpaintings are used to cure sick people. It is believed they help the healer to find the cause of the sickness from the Holy People who live in the sky. First he clears the floor of a hut. Then he paints the figures of Father Sky and Mother Earth, using sand, flower pollen, and charcoal. Finally, a line of corn pollen is trickled between the figures. It represents the sacred path said to lead the patient to harmony and good health.

HEAVENLY BUILDINGS

If you were to design a building that would give a glimpse of Heaven on Earth, what would you choose? Would it be a palace made of silver or a castle of gleaming gold? It would need to be beautiful, that's for sure. Over the centuries, people have built many breathtaking buildings as places of worship and to glorify God. Even if you do not have strong beliefs, sitting for a moment in a great temple or cathedral can fill you with a sense of heavenly peace and awe.

MARBLE MEMORIAL

THE Taj Mahal in India was built by the Mughal emperor Shah Jahan in memory of his wife Mumtaz who died in 1631. Heartbroken, the emperor summoned architects, masons, and craftsmen from all over the world to build the most magnificent tomb ever seen. The white marble Taj stands on a raised platform at the end of formal gardens, thought to match the design of the gardens of Heaven described in the Qur'an. And carved around the gateway as you enter the gardens are the beautiful words, "Enter thou My Paradise" from the Qur'an.

The Taj Mahal in India.

THE GOLDEN TEMPLE

THE Sikhs' holiest shrine is the Golden Temple in Amritsar, India. It stands, gleaming and glittering, in the middle of a holy lake. Sikhs bathe in the water and believe it will help them to live forever. The golden walls of the temple are covered with passages from the *Guru Granth Sahib*. Inside is a copy of this sacred book. It is a beautiful place, and for Sikhs, crossing the causeway to the temple is a bit like crossing from Earth to Heaven.

HEAVENLY SPIRES

THE great cathedrals of the Middle Ages were built to sing God's praises and glory. Because Heaven was thought to be up in the sky, they had towering spires which soared elegantly upwards. The cathedrals were covered in magnificent sculptures and carvings which were masterpieces of the stonemason's art. The builders took great pride in their work for they saw it as a way of asking forgiveness for their sins and of reaching Heaven.

Chartres Cathedral, France.

THE TEMPLE OF HEAVEN

THE Temple of Heaven in Beijing, China, (right) was built as a personal temple for the emperor, who was known as the Son of Heaven. Here he prayed to Shang-Ti, the god of Heaven and to the other heavenly spirits who controlled the sun, moon, clouds, and rain. The temple itself is circular, built in the image of Heaven. It is painted blue, the color of Heaven. It stands in a square, representing the Earth, to mark the joining of Earth and Heaven.

"Heaven is a castle in the sky. It is made out of sunflowers so bright they shine like gold. When people go to Heaven, they turn into angels and live in the castle."

**Yolanda Black Fuentes
aged 10**

To Heaven and Back

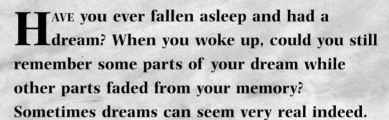

HAVE you ever fallen asleep and had a dream? When you woke up, could you still remember some parts of your dream while other parts faded from your memory? Sometimes dreams can seem very real indeed. Some people say that they have been to Heaven in their dreams. Others claim to have actually died, gone to Heaven and come back to Earth again, having had a brief glimpse of what lies beyond. Others claim to have met with angels or talked to the spirits. But are their experiences real, or are they dreams too? No one really knows. Often their memories of what they saw are very similar. Can they all be wrong? Or are some dreams of Heaven so strong you truly feel that you have been there? Can we ever prove that Heaven is more than a dream?

JOURNEY TO HEAVEN

WHAT will Heaven be like? And how do we get there? Does anyone ever come back? Some people say that they know the answers from first-hand experience. They claim to have left their bodies for a short time and experienced Heaven. But are their experiences real, or are they more likely to be journeys of the imagination? Many scientists dismiss them as powerful dreams or hallucinations. But to the people involved, their visits to Heaven and the wonderful things they saw and felt there seem very real indeed.

NEAR DEATH

AN NDE, or Near Death Experience, is when people think they have died and come back to life. They can remember their soul or life force leaving their body and their return to life. Many NDEs happen when people are very ill or close to dying. Whether they are dreams or real journeys, people who have had NDEs often find their lives transformed. The experience comforts them because it shows them not to be afraid of death. It also gives their lives greater meaning, making them keen to live each day to the full, now that they have been given a second chance.

Strange is it not? that of the myriads who
Before us passed the door of Darkness through,
Not one returns to tell us of the Road,
Which to discover we must travel too.

The Rubaiyat of Omar Khayyam

LIGHT AT THE END OF THE TUNNEL

MANY reports of NDEs are amazingly similar. For example, the people feel they are floating above their physical body, watching what is happening below. Then they are drawn down a long, dark tunnel towards a bright shining light. At the end of the tunnel, friends and relatives who have already died come to meet them. They see their lives flash before their eyes as if caught on film. Many people feel such an incredible sense of joy and love that it makes it difficult to leave. They want to stay but return for the sake of their loved ones. So, could these experiences *all* be wrong, or does the fact that they are so similar mean that there must be some truth in them? Was this Heaven?

ASTRAL TRAVELING

SOME people say that they have another body, apart from their physical one. This is called an astral body into which their soul moves when people die. It is then thought to travel to the astral plane, a world similar to Earth but where time stands still and where there is no pain or suffering, only a great feeling of love. A world which sounds very much like Heaven. It is believed that an astral body moves into this world, just for a short time, while people are sleeping. So dying may be as simple and peaceful as going to sleep.

At first, when the light came,
I wasn't sure what was happening, but then it
asked me if I was ready to die. It was like talking to a
person but the person wasn't there. The light was what
was talking to me . . . From the moment the light spoke
to me, I felt really good – secure and loved.

Raymond Moody
Life After Life

127

GHOSTS AND HAUNTINGS

FLOATING white shapes, strange whisperings, footsteps on the stairs, things that go bump in the night, all these may be signs of a ghostly presence. But what are ghosts? Some people say that ghosts don't exist. They are simply your imagination playing tricks, especially if you are on your own, at night or in a spooky place. In other words, ghosts are all in the mind. But many other people claim that ghosts do exist, and that seeing is believing . . .

WANDERING SPIRITS

IF ghosts do exist, what are they and where do they come from? Many people believe that ghosts are the restless souls of the dead, destined to wander on Earth. Perhaps they are trapped between worlds. In ancient times, this terrible fate was thought likely if a person was not given a proper religious funeral and could not rest in peace. Ghosts do not always have good intentions. Some are said to return to Earth to take revenge or cause mischief. Have you seen a ghost? Perhaps you have but you didn't realize it at the time? After all, not all ghosts wear white sheets, hold their heads under their arms or float through walls!

BUMP IN THE NIGHT

THE word *poltergeist* means "noisy spirit" and noisy these ghosts certainly are. These are believed to be the mischievous ghosts which make things go bump in the night. They seem to enjoy opening doors and windows, moving furniture around, and sending objects flying across the room. Some people even claim to have been pinched or punched by spiteful poltergeists! Investigators say that all this activity is the poltergeists' way of trying to communicate with the living. But what they are trying to say, nobody knows.

"There are ghosts in our house because they keep stealing the cookies. And my mother keeps blaming me!"

Ellie
aged 9

HAUNTED HOUSES

WHEN a ghost keeps appearing in the same place, such as a house, church, or castle, that building is said to be haunted. This may be where the dead person lived or died, or a place with strong, often tragic, emotional ties. Sometimes the ghost is a famous person, such as a king or queen. But phantom animals, vehicles and even whole armies have also been seen. Almost any building can be haunted. One of the most famous is the White House in Washington DC, the official residence of the American President. One of its most frequent ghostly visitors is the former president, Abraham Lincoln. But he isn't the only ghost to be seen there!

MAKING CONTACT

SOME people claim to have a special "sixth sense" which allows them to see into the future or make contact with another world. These people are called psychic. Some, called mediums, claim to be able to bring messages from the spirit world. Some mediums help people make contact with a loved one. Others try to help ghosts find their way out of this world to the next. Some people do not believe in these powers, and many mediums have been found to be false.

129

PAST LIVes

WHO were you in a past life? Who would you have *liked* to be? An Egyptian princess, a famous artist or explorer or a knight in shining armor? Many people believe that when you die, you are born again in another body. This is called reincarnation (see pages 20, 34). It is an important belief in many ancient religions. So you might already have lived on Earth several times before. Just imagine that! Have you ever had the feeling that someone you meet or somewhere you visit is familiar to you but you don't know quite why? This may be because you are remembering something from one of your past lives.

ME

by Walter de la Mare

As long as I live
I shall always be
My Self – and no
other,
Just me.

Like a tree –
Willow, elder,
Aspen, thorn,
Or cypress forlorn.

Like a flower,
For its hour –

Primrose, or pink,
Or a violet –
Sunned by the sun,
And with dewdrops
wet.

Always just me.
Till the day come on
When I leave this
body,
It's all then done,
And the spirit within it
Is gone.

130

LOOKING BACK

IN recent years, some people have become very interested in finding out more about their past lives. Some believe that this can help treat illnesses, such as phobias, fears, and sleeplessness because these are carried over from the past. Different techniques are used to guide these persons back. Under hypnosis, they are asked to imagine a stairway or a tunnel, leading them into the past. Once there, they might identify with a particular figure, often a person with an ordinary job, like a farmer or a shopkeeper. Then they try to change their attitudes about what happened in the past so that they are no longer affected by them.

FACT OR FALSE MEMORY?

UNDER hypnosis, some people are able to remember the past in extraordinary detail, right down to the clothes they were wearing or the food they were eating. Some can even speak a foreign language, even though they have never spoken it before. So are they really remembering their own lives? Some people say that they are simply remembering things they have read in books or seen on the television. After all, our brains are constantly storing information, even if we can't remember it all.

For Buddhists, the bodhisattava, Avalokiteshvara is reborn as His Holiness the Dalai Lama.

DÉJÀ VU

Have you ever had the strangest feeling that you have been in a situation before? For example, you might be having a conversation with someone and suddenly realize you have had the same conversation with the same person before. This feeling is called *déjà vu* which is French for "seen before." It lasts for a second and then it is gone. Some people think that déjà vu is a memory from a past life. What about you?

DALAI LAMA

BUDDHISTS in Tibet believe that their leader, the Dalai Lama, is the reincarnation of the *bodhisattva*, Avalokiteshvara. When the old lama dies, the monks set out on their search for his successor, usually still a baby. It is a long and difficult process, leading them all over Tibet. Sometimes the previous Dalai Lama leaves clues to follow. Sometimes the monks consult the sacred lake, Lhamo Lhatso, famous for the visions that appear in its waters. The baby must look like the Dalai Lama and be able to identify some of his possessions without any help. If he can, he is brought to Lhasa (Tibet's capital) to be trained and taught his new duties.

"Last week we went to visit a big, posh stately home. It was spooky because I thought I'd been there before. But my mum said I hadn't."

**Marcus
aged 10**

Visions of Hell

IF you don't make it to Heaven, some people believe you might end up in the other place, Hell, instead. In every way, Hell is the very opposite of Heaven, a dark, frightening place far away from heavenly light and happiness. It was sometimes thought of as a place where wicked people were sent to be punished while good people earned their rewards in Heaven. Worse still, it was far away from the joy of God's presence and love. This is why, in the past, Hell was often used as a way of scaring people into behaving better or following their faith more diligently. But many other things can be hellish too, such as wars or terrible diseases. On a personal level, being lonely or sad can feel like being in Hell. Everyone's Hell is different.

WHERE IS HELL?

WHERE is Hell? And what it is like? Nobody really knows. But that hasn't stopped people letting their imaginations run wild. Hell was often seen as a terrible place underground, deep beneath the Earth, about as far away from the lofty heights of Heaven as you could possibly get. It was sometimes baking hot, sometimes freezing cold, or both, and it was usually dark, smelly and horribly overcrowded – not a very pleasant place to be! As for getting to Hell, that was thought to be easy – being thoroughly nasty and wicked would do. And getting out again? Well, that was much, much harder . . .

FIRE AND BRIMSTONE

IN the past, Christians imagined Hell as a terrifying place full of pain and suffering. Woe betide them if they led a sinful life on Earth. In Hell, they would get their punishment! Early pictures of Hell were very vivid, and frightening. They often showed a place of torment where the wicked were burned by fire or tortured by evil demons. Today, many Christians do not believe in Hell as a real place. For them, it is a symbol of the terrible feelings of loss and unhappiness they suffer if they are separated from God's love.

"I don't believe in Hell being full of fire. I've been down in the ground and I've never seen any fire."

**Billy Kennedy
aged 8**

IN LIMBO

HAVE you heard the phrase "in limbo"? It means to be caught between two things. In ancient beliefs, limbo (meaning "on the border") lay between Heaven and Hell. It was a place people went to if they didn't quite fit in Heaven or Hell. It wasn't as horrible as Hell nor as joyful as Heaven. Some Christians believe in a kind of limbo called purgatory, a place where souls were given one last chance to make themselves worthy to enter Heaven. Saying prayers for these unfortunate souls could help shorten their stay in purgatory.

THE HORRIBLE PIT

"ON that day, there will be downcast faces of people broken and worn out, burnt by a scorching fire and drinking from a boiling fountain. Their only food will be bitter thorns." This verse from the Qur'an describes the fate that awaits those Muslims who do not obey Allah in their earthly lives. On the Day of Judgement, they would plummet down to the vast, fiery pit of Hell. It was a dreadful place but it might not last for ever. Muslims believe that Allah is merciful and if they are truly sorry for their sins, they might be pardoned and, one day, reach Paradise.

(Right) A famous painting called The Scream by Edvard Munch

134

HELL ON EARTH

HAVE you ever had a very bad day when nothing seemed to go right? Or felt guilty because you have done something wrong and can't tell anyone about it? There are many ways of creating Hell on Earth. It might be as simple as having too much homework to do, or as serious as a natural disaster or war. It might be being deliberately spiteful or cruel, or making someone else's life a misery. A famous writer once said that Hell was other people. You might have your own ideas. What would Hell on Earth be like for you?

...so shall it be in the end of this world. The Son of man shall send forth his angels, and they shall gather out of his kingdom all things that offend, and them which do iniquity; and shall cast them into a furnace of fire: there will be wailing and gnashing of teeth.

St Matthew 13 verses 40-43

Ancient Hells

THERE are many different ideas and beliefs about Hell. These often reflect people's deepest worries and fears. Whatever their differences of opinion, though they all agree about one thing though – that Hell is a place best avoided!

ETERNAL PUNISHMENTS

THE Ancient Greek Hell was called Tartarus, part of the Underworld, Hades (see p. 86). This was not normally believed to be a place of punishment, except for people who had been especially bad. Imagine having to wash the dishes or tidy your room over and over again. A hellish thought. A similar punishment was given to a king called Sisyphus for crimes against Zeus, king of the gods. He was condemned to roll a huge stone up a steep hill. Every time, just as he reached the top, the stone rolled back down and he was forced to start all over again! Another king, Tantalus, was made to reach for food and drink, which was always just beyond his grasp. This is how we get the word to tantalize, meaning to tease.

"I think Hell has a floor made of red hot iron bars. It has massive black gates. In the centre of Hell the devil sits on a throne of human heads."

**Patrick Brown
aged 10**

HOPE IN HELL

In Buddhist beliefs, it is believed that people may go to Hell if they've behaved badly on Earth. The good news is that this stay does not last for ever, only until the person's next rebirth. The bad news is that some Buddhists believe in not one, but eight, main hells, with many lesser hells attached. Each hell has its own set of punishments. There are hells of fire, fumes, dung, and of burning hot ashes. Or there is the hell of crushing, or screaming, or repetition, or the hell of trees with swords for leaves. Ouch!

THE LAND OF DARKNESS

In the Shinto religion of Japan, the land of darkness beneath the Earth was the home of the demons which cause bad luck, accidents, illnesses, and unhappiness, in fact all of the problems which affect the human world above. This land was called Yomi. To be protected from these demons, a prayer had to be said or an offering made to Kamu Nahobi, the god who puts things right again. Later, Hell was imagined as eight worlds of fire and eight worlds of ice, ruled over by the Great Judge of Hell who judged people's souls and handed out suitably nasty punishments.

JOURNEY TO HELL

Do you remember the story of the Shinto gods, Izanagi and Izanami, and how they created the world? You can read about them on page 60. Here is more of their story. For many years, Izanagi and Izanami lived happily on Earth and had lots of children. But then tragedy struck. Izanami died giving birth to her last child, the god of fire. Izanagi was inconsolable. Without his beloved wife, life did not seem worth living. He decided to visit the land of darkness and bring her back to life again. Izanami met Izanagi at the gateway to Yomi but she refused to return to Earth with him. She decided to ask the god of death's advice but she warned Izanagi to wait where he was, and not to follow her into Hell. Then she disappeared into the darkness.

Izanagi waited for a very long time. Soon he couldn't wait any longer. Then he broke a tooth off the comb he wore in his hair and, using it as a torch, he went after Izanami. A hideous sight met his eyes – Izanami's body rotting and riddled with worms. Izanagi ran away as fast as possible, followed by hundreds of Hell's ugly demons. As soon as he could, he dived into the sea to wash away the memory of what he had seen.

WHO LIVES IN HELL?

In some beliefs, Hell is thought to be full of scary devils and demons whose job is to make life a misery. They stand for evil and unhappiness, the very opposite of the angels in Heaven. There are gods and goddesses of Hell, too, with armies of demons as their servants. Some people think that all of us have our personal demons, things or feelings inside us which we don't want to face up to. Bringing them out into the open can make them seem less frightening. For example, you might have done something wrong and be too scared to own up.

DEVIL'S DELIGHTS

In many beliefs, the ruler of Hell is known as the Devil. You've probably seen pictures of the Devil, with horns, hooves, red skin like flames and a forked tail, a cross between a demon and a dragon. His scary features showed people just how wicked he could be. For the Devil was believed to be God's arch enemy, the cause of all the evils and problems in the world. If anything went wrong, the Devil was to blame. Or Ilbis, or Satan, or Beelzebub, to list some of the Devil's other names.

> "I called the devil, and he came;
> With wonder his form did I closely scan;
> He is not ugly and is not lame,
> But really a handsome and charming man."
>
> **Heinrich Heine**
> *Travel Sketches*

HELL'S ANGELS

IT is said that Satan was once an angel in Heaven, the closest archangel to God and the most beautiful. His name was Lucifer, bringer of light. One story says that when God made Adam, the first man, he asked Lucifer to bow before him to show his respect. But Lucifer was too proud and refused. So God cast him out of Heaven and a third of the angels with him. Then Lucifer led his forces in a war against Heaven but was defeated and hurled down into the pit of Hell. Here he became Satan, the prince of darkness and evil.

HEL'S HELL

IN Viking mythology, Hel was the name of a gruesome goddess who ruled over the land of the dead. From the waist up, she looked like a beautiful woman; from the waist down, a hideous skeleton. Hel's kingdom was called Niflheim, a grim, icy place, shrouded in eternal mist and darkness. The entrance was guarded by a ferocious dog, called Garm, who made sure that no one escaped.

Hel was the daughter of Loki, the god of mischief, and a gigantess. In the final battle (see p.82), it was thought that she and her brother, the wolf, Fenrir, would lead the dead against the gods.

SLAYING DEMONS

AT Chinese New Year, some people hang up pictures of a very special person whom they believe will protect their homes from demons. This is Chung K'ui, the demon slayer. Legend says that Chung K'ui's ghost once saved the emperor from being attacked by a demon. As a reward, Chung K'ui was named official demon slayer for the empire and given a tiger to ride on and an army of spirits to help him with his work.

hist wist
by E.E. Cummings

hist   whist
little ghostthings
tip-toe
twinkle-toe

little twitchy
witches and tingling
goblins
hob-a-nob   hob-a-hob

little hoppy happy
toad in tweeds
tweeds
little itchy mousies

with scuttling
eyes   rustle and run   and
hidehidehide
whisk

whisk   look out for the old woman
with the wart on her nose
what she'll do to yer
nobody knows

for she knows the devil   ooch
the devil   ouch
the devil
ach   the great

green
dancing
devil
devil

devil
devil

        wheeEEE

GATES OF HELL

HAVE **you ever wondered what lies underground, deep beneath your feet? Perhaps you have been into a cave and wondered where it led? Scientists now know a great deal about the Earth but ancient people could only guess. For them, the underground world was a dark, gloomy, mysterious place, a fitting place for the land of the dead. And caves, caverns, cracks in the ground, springs and violent volcanoes were all believed to be the gateways that led to Hell. Of course, the gates of Hell may lie somewhere else entirely – perhaps the gates leading into your school! Do you have any other ideas?**

HELL FIRE

ANCIENT people who lived near volcanoes treated them with great fear and awe. They believed that the gods lived inside their craters and that when the volcanoes erupted, it meant the gods were angry, very angry. Then the fireworks really began. When a volcano erupted, the Earth itself seemed to split apart and spit out fire and flames. No wonder that they believed that it must be extremely hot underground, and that the volcanoes were the entrances to the fiery pits of Hell.

*There
is a dreadful Hell,
And everlasting pains;
There sinners must with devils dwell
In darkness, fire, and chains.*

Isaac Watts
Divine Songs for Children

The eruption of Stromboli, a volcano in Italy.

HELL UNDER THE LAKE

In his famous poem, the *Aeneid*, the Roman writer Virgil claimed that the entrance to Hell lay deep under Lake Avernus, near Naples in Italy. This was certainly a spooky enough place. The landscape around the lake is volcanic, with pools of mud bubbling up from the ground, and everywhere the stinky smell of sulphur. Whisps of steam and fumes rise from the waters of the lake itself. Who knows what lies beneath them? A church now stands near the lake. It is called Santa Maria del Inferno, or St. Mary of the Fire.

STORY OF AENEAS

The hills around Lake Avernus are pitted with caves, also believed by some to lead to Hell. The most famous is the cave of the Cumaean Sibyl, an ancient Greek prophetess. According to Greek legend, it was she who guided Aeneas, the hero of the *Aeneid*, to the kingdom of the dead and back again. Aeneas wanted to go to Hell to visit the spirit of his father which kept appearing to him in dreams. The Sibyl led him into Hell, a terrible place full of sorrow, lies, and lost souls. Finally, they reached the golden palace of Pluto, king of the dead, and met Aeneas's father. Those who descend into the Underworld do not normally leave. But Aeneas had a golden branch cut from a sacred tree and so was able to return to Earth.

UNDERWORLD WATERS

Beneath the Earth's surface lies a layer of water, formed from rain which has seeped underground. In places, the water bubbles up again, forming gushing springs. Because they come from deep beneath the ground, many people used to believe that they came from the Underworld and so had magical powers. Their water could make wishes come true, grant wisdom or give the gift of immortality. Some believed they could even bring the dead back to life. But springs were also dangerous places. If a person fell into one, they might plunge into the Underworld and never come back again.

Tales from Hell

HELL, **for many people, is scary, fascinating and mysterious – a perfect subject for a gripping story. There are many tales about Hell and what might happen there. In the past, these were used to explain bad things that happened and to warn readers or listeners to be good. Some told of people who visited the Underworld and came back to Earth again. Others tell of travelers who were not so lucky. They went to Hell, and stayed there . . .**

How Winter came

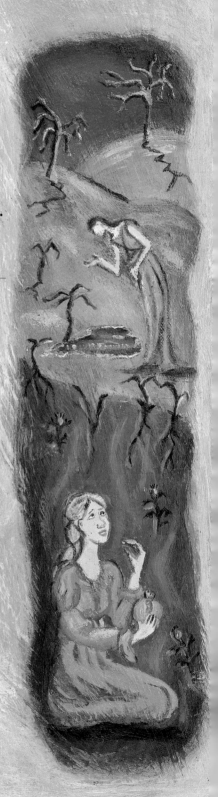

THIS Ancient Greek story tells how winter came to the world. Demeter the Greek goddess of plants and crops, had a beautiful daughter, Persephone. One day, Persephone was picking flowers in the woods when she saw a bright yellow narcissus. But as she bent down to pick it, a huge hole opened in the ground and swallowed Persephone up. She found herself deep beneath the Earth, in the kingdom of Pluto, god of the dead.

When Demeter realized that her daughter was gone, she was beside herself with grief. She could not sleep, or eat, or rest. She neglected the crops and left the fields bare. Soon there would be no food to eat. The gods begged Demeter to change her mind. Finally, Zeus, the mighty king of the gods, sent his messenger to fetch Persephone back. Demeter was overjoyed, and the world burst once again into bloom.

But Persephone could not stay on Earth for ever. In the Underworld she had eaten six seeds from a pomegranate, and so she had to return to Hades. Zeus took pity on Persephone.

"You will spend part of the year in Hades," he said. "And the rest on Earth with your mother."

And this is how winter came to the world. While Persephone is in the Underworld, the land lies barren. When she returns, life returns to the world and it is spring.

ONE LAST LOOK

THIS story may have been told to help people accept that death is an inevitable part of life. It cannot be undone, however hard you wish.

Another Greek hero, Orpheus, visited the Underworld to beg Pluto to free his beloved wife, Eurydice. She had died from a snakebite. Orpheus was the best musician in Greece and played so beautifully on his lyre that Pluto granted his wish. But he must lead her from the Underworld without looking back. Orpheus set off and Eurydice followed. But the temptation was too great. Orpheus looked back and lost Eurydice for ever.

THE HUNGRY GHOSTS

THERE was once a monk, called Mu-lien, a follower of the Buddha. Mu-lien had to go on a long journey. Before he left, he gave his mother some money to give to the monks who came to her door. But his greedy mother kept the money for herself and lied to her son when he returned. Because of this, when she died, she went straight to Hell.

Now Mu-lien was a kind, wise man. He set off for Hell to rescue his mother. On the way he met Yama, god of death, who told him that no one could save her now.

"Her crime was so serious," Yama said. "We sent her to the deepest part of Hell to teach her a lesson."

Mu-lien journeyed down and down. On the way, a gang of fifty bull-headed demons attacked him but he waved them away with his magic wand, a gift from the Buddha. Finally, he found his mother in a tiny cell, tied to a bed with long, strong chains. Only the Buddha had the power to save her.

So Mu-lien begged the Buddha for help, and because of his goodness, the Buddha agreed.

"But, each year," he said, "your mother must make a feast for the monks to make up for her meanness. Then and only then she can go free."

And every year, Mu-lien's mother cooked for the monks, on a day which became known as the Festival of the Hungry Ghosts. She always saved some food for these ghosts who were doomed to wander for ever through the depths of Hell.

143

HELL ON EARTH

WHAT is your own idea of Hell? Some people say that Hell is not an actual place or something which only happens when you die. Hell can happen right here on Earth. It might be something niggling or annoying, like having too much homework or, for your parents, getting stuck in traffic on the way to work. It might be something much more serious, the bad things that happen in the world, like wars, diseases, famine, and prejudice. These can create Hell on Earth, and bring their own modern devils. The important thing to remember is that even if we find ourselves in a hellish situation or in a hell of our making, there is a way out. We can find it if we decide to do something about the situation and face up to bad things in our lives.

LIFE AND DEATH

MANY people say that their idea of Heaven is to be fit and well. Staying healthy is very important to us, as is the health of our friends and family. So falling seriously ill can be devastating. Diseases such as cancer and AIDS (Acquired Immune Deficiency Syndrome) claim millions of lives every year. Doctors and scientists all over the world are working hard to develop new medicines, and maybe to find a cure. They have not found one yet but they are making good progress and there is hope for a cure in the future.

NATURAL DISASTERS

WHEN earthquakes, hurricanes, volcanic eruptions, and other natural disasters strike, it can certainly seem like Hell on Earth. There is often very little that people can do to stop nature's fury. When Hurricane Mitch hit Central America in 1998, it left tens of thousands of people with nothing: no homes, or work, or food. Large parts of the region were simply washed away, and people are still trying to rebuild their lives. To make matters worse, the places and people who suffer most are often among the poorest in the world. They do not have the money or resources to cope.

People in Central America had a glimpse of Hell when Hurricane Mitch devastated their countries. Here a survivor stands by a collapsed road.

THE HOLOCAUST

DURING World War II, millions of Jews and other minority groups in Europe suffered Hell on Earth. Persecuted by the German Nazis, under the leadership of Adolf Hitler, they were taken from their homes, rounded up, and sent to concentration camps. Millions were murdered in the gas chambers. Those that survived suffered a living Hell. Many felt guilty that they had survived when so many of their friends and relatives had died. This dreadful event was called the Holocaust. In total, some six million Jews were killed. And still today, racial and religious prejudice and intolerance make a misery of many people's lives.

It's utterly impossible for me to build my life on a foundation of chaos, suffering and death. I see the world being slowly transformed into a wilderness, I hear the approaching thunder that one day will destroy us too. I feel the suffering of millions. And yet, when I look up at the sky, I somehow feel that everything will change for the better, that this cruelty too will end, that peace and tranquility will return once more. In the meantime, I must hold on to my ideals. Perhaps the day will come when I'll be able to realize them!

Anne Frank
The Diary of a Young Girl

FUTURE HELL

WHAT does the future hold? What are the dangers facing the world? Some people are worried about the use of nuclear weapons and fear that they will trigger another world war. If this happened, they say, the world would be destroyed. The radioactive particles, dust, and smoke released into the atmosphere would create a vast cloud over the planet, blocking out the Sun. In this so-called nuclear winter, plants, animals, and people would die of cold. But it's not all doom and gloom. Many countries are now working hard to try to make sure that this never happens.

Jews being rounded up by the Nazis.

WHAT DO YOU THINK?

*Ah, but a man's reach should exceed
his grasp,
Or what's a heaven for*

Robert Browning

Now that you have read all about Heaven, what
do you think? Have you found a big answer to
the big question? Do you think that Heaven could be
a real place, or is it more likely to be a state of mind,
something to dream of and live up to? Can we only
reach Heaven when we die or should we try our best
to create Heaven on Earth? And is it up to you to
create your own Heaven, or is this someone else's job,
like a priest's, or your parents', or the politicians'? Or
is the whole point of Heaven that here is a question
to which the answer can never be known?

ONE thing is certain, there are a great many ways of thinking about Heaven and a great many ways of getting there. Even within the same religion, people have different hopes and beliefs. Despite this, there are many heavenly features in common. For example, Heaven is often pictured as a beautiful, peaceful place and opposed to the darkness and misery of Hell. These pictures did not happen by accident. They are deliberately and carefully drawn to give us something to aspire to, and keep us on our toes!

BECAUSE no one has been to Heaven and returned to tell us what they saw, we can never know for certain what Heaven is like. So your own Heaven can be what you want it to be, a fabulous mixture of all your hopes, dreams, favorite people and things. What could be more heavenly than that!

GLOSSARY

Allah The Muslim name for God. Muslims believe that Allah is the one true God who created the world and everything in it.

Amaterasu-o-Mikami The Shinto goddess of the Sun

Amitabha A Buddha who lives in a Heaven called the Pure Land

Ame Heaven in Shinto belief

Ancestors Your relations who have died before you

Angel A heavenly being who lives close to God but sometimes brings messages to Earth.

Astral body The part of you that exists in the astral plane

Astral plane A spiritual world close to the physical Earth but separate from it

Astrology The study of the sun, moon, stars and planets and how they may influence our lives and behaviour

Astronomy The scientific study of space and the heavenly bodies (stars, planets, moons, comets and so on)

Avalon A heavenly place said to have existed in England in ancient times and where King Arthur may be buried

Avatars In Hindu belief, the shapes or bodies that gods or goddesses take when they visit the Earth

Baha'i A religion which began in Persia (now Iran) in the nineteenth century. Its followers are called Baha'is.

Baha'u'llah One of the first teachers of the Baha'i religion. He taught that all people and religions are equal.

BCE Stands for Before the Common Era. It is used to write dates which happened before the year 0.

Bible The holy book of the Christian religion. It consists of the Old Testament and the New Testament.

Bodhisattva For some Buddhists, an enlightened being who could enter nirvana but chooses to be reborn in order to help others to reach enlightenment too

Brahman In Hindu belief, the great soul or spirit who is sometimes known as God. Brahman is everywhere, in everything.

Buddha The title given to an Indian nobleman, Siddhartha Gautama, when he achieved enlightenment. It means enlightened or awakened one.

Buddhism A system of beliefs based on the teachings of the Buddha.

Cathedral A large, important Christian church which is looked after by a bishop

CE Stands for Common Era. It is used to write dates which happened after the year 0.

Charon In Ancient Greek legend, the ferryman who rowed the souls of the dead across the River Styx to Hades

Ch'i In Chinese belief, an invisible energy or life force said to flow through your body and through the world

Christian A follower of the Christian religion

Christianity A religion based on the teachings of Jesus Christ. Jesus's life and teaching were written about in the New Testament of the Bible.

Confucius A Chinese philosopher who lived in the sixth century BCE. He gave up his government job to teach people how to live in peace.

Creation The making of the world. There are many stories about how the world was created.

Dalai Lama The title of the leader of Tibet's Buddhists. It means ocean of wisdom. Because of Tibet's political situation, the present Dalai Lama lives in exile in India.

Darshana In Hindu belief, a sight or viewing of a sacred image in a mandir. The image represents the presence of a god or goddess.

Day of the Dead A Mexican festival on which the souls of the dead are believed to return, very briefly, to Earth

Déjà Vu When something seems strangely familar, as if you have seen it or experienced it before

Demon An evil spirit or devil

Dreaming, the In Aborigine belief, a time long ago when the world was made

Enlightenment Like waking up from a long, deep sleep and being able to see and understand the true meaning of life

Extraterrestrial A being from another planet other than Earth. Often shortened to ET.

Feng Shui The ancient Chinese practice of living in harmony with nature and the Earth

Gabriel An important angel for Christians, Muslims and Jews. Muslims call him Jibril .

Gaia Theory The idea that the Earth is a living, growing being that we should treat well and care for

Ganges The most important river in India. For Hindus, its waters are sacred. They believe that it can wash away sins.

God In many beliefs, a great, all-knowing power who created and rules over the world

Guardian angel An angel believed to look after you throughout your life

Gurdwara A building where Sikhs meet to worship

Guru Nanak The founder of the Sikh religion and the first Sikh Guru or teacher. He lived from 1469-1539 in India.

Hades The Greek Underworld, an underground kingdom where the souls of the dead went

Hajj The pilgrimage to Makkah which all Muslims try to make at least once in their lifetimes

Hallucination Seeing things which are not really there

Hindu Someone who follows the Hindu religion or Hinduism

Hinduism The ancient religion of India which began about 4,000 years ago

Holocaust The name given to the mass murder of Jews by the Nazis in World War II

Holy Ark The special cupboard in a synagogue where the Torah scrolls are kept

Horoscope A chart which shows the positions of the stars and planets at the time of your birth

Icon A painting which shows a portrait of Jesus or a saint. Icons are used as a focus of worship in the Orthodox Church.

Immortal Living for ever

Incense A sweet-smelling stick or cone often burnt in temples and other sacred places

Inuit The name given to the native people who live around the Arctic Ocean. Inuit means 'the People' in their own language.

Islam The religion of the Muslims. The word Islam means 'obedience'.

Jacob In the Torah and Old Testament of the Bible, the son of Isaac, one of the early leaders of the Jews

Jade Emperor In Chinese belief, the ruler of Heaven

Jah The Rastafarian name for God

Jains People who follow the Jain religion which began in India about 2,500 years ago

Jatakas Stories told about the Buddha's past lives in which he often appears as a animal to teach a particular moral or lesson

Jesus A teacher and healer who lived about 2,000 years ago in Israel. Christians believe that Jesus was the Son of God.

Jew Someone who follows the Jewish religion, or Judaism

Jibril See Gabriel

Judaism The religion of the Jewish people. According to Jewish scriptures, the first Jew was Abraham who lived some 4,000 years ago.

Judgement Day In Christian, Muslim and some Jewish belief, a day on which God will bring the dead back to life and judge them according to their good or bad deeds. Then they will be sent to Heaven or Hell.

Kaddish An ancient Jewish prayer

Kami In Shinto belief, the gods or spirits which live in people, animals, plants and natural features

Karma The idea that all your actions, good or bad have good or bad consequences which affect your next life. An important belief for Hindus, Buddhists and Jains.

Krishna A popular Hindu god often shown with blue or black skin. Krishna is an avatar of the god Vishnu.

Ley lines Invisible lines of energy said to run across the Earth's surface, linking sacred places

Lucifer Satan's name when he lived in Heaven as an angel

Mahavira A holy man who lived in India about 2,500 years ago. He was the last and greatest of the Jain teachers.

Makkah (Mecca) A city in Saudi Arabia which is holy for Muslims. It is where the Prophet Muhammad was born.

Mandala A circular picture which some Buddhists use to help them meditate

Mandir A place where Hindus worship. It is also called a temple.

Mecca *See* Makkah

Meditation To focus or concentrate your mind on just one thought, or to clear your mind of all thoughts. This helps to make you feel peaceful and calm.

Medium A person who acts as a messenger between this world and the spirit world

Messiah A promised leader. Christians believe that Jesus was the promised messiah.

Millennium A period of one thousand years said to begin with the birth of Jesus which is traditionally given as the year 0

Moksha In Hindu belief, freedom from the cycle of birth, death and rebirth

Moses An early Jewish leader who led the Jews out of slavery in Egypt. According to scripture, God appeared to Moses on Mount Sinai and gave him the Ten Commandments.

Mosque A building where Muslims meet to worship

Muhammad In Muslim belief, the last and greatest of the prophets sent by Allah to teach people how to live

Mukti In Sikh belief, salvation or freedom from the cycle of birth, death and rebirth

Mount Meru In Hindu and Jain belief, a mythical mountain said to mark the centre of the Universe

Mount Sinai A mountain in Egypt. In Jewish and Christian belief, the mountain on which God appeared to Moses to give him the Ten Commandments.

Near Death Experience When a person thinks that they have died and then come back to life again. It is called an NDE, for short.

New Age A wide range of beliefs in which healing and care for the environment and everything in it are very important

Nirvana In Buddhist belief, a state of perfect peace and happiness reached by people who achieve enlightenment

O-bon A Japanese festival on which the spirits of the dead are welcomed back home just for a short time

Philosopher Someone who studies the meaning of life, nature, science and beliefs

Poltergeist A mischievous ghost that makes noises or moves objects about

Prayer A way of talking to God or to the spirits, perhaps to ask for help or say thank you for something

Prophet In Judaism, Christianity and Islam, someone chosen by God to speak to people about God's wishes for the world

Purgatory In some Christian belief, a place of suffering where souls may spend some time before entering Heaven

Psychic A psychic person is someone who claims to have special powers which allow them to make contact with the spirit world

Qur'an The holy book of the Muslims. Muslims believe that it contains Allah's very words.

Rabbi A Jewish religious teacher

Rama A popular Hindu god, worshipped for his courage and goodness. Rama is an avatar of the god Vishnu.

Rastafarianism A religion which began in Jamaica, West Indies, in the 1930s. It mixes Christian and African beliefs.

Rebirth Being born again when you die, in a different body

Reggae A type of music with a strong, catchy beat which is part of Rastafarian culture. It often uses themes from the Bible.

Reincarnation *See* rebirth

Resurrection Coming back to life again from the dead. The resurrection of Jesus is particularly important for Christians.

Sabbath For Jews and Christians, a holy day of rest and worship each week. The Jewish Sabbath or Shabbat lasts from sunset on Friday to sunset on Saturday.

Sacred Another word for holy

Samsara In Hindu and Buddhist belief, the cycle of birth, death and rebirth

Satan In Christian and Muslim belief, God's arch enemy who causes sin and evil in the world. He is also called the Devil.

Shaman A type of priest whose soul is believed to be able to travel between this world and the spirit world where he speaks to the spirits on people's behalfs.

Shinto An ancient religion from Japan. Its followers worship spirits called kami.

Shiva One of the three main Hindu gods. Shiva is the destroyer of evil in the Universe.

Shraddha A Hindu ceremony held on the anniversary of a person's death

Sikh A follower of the Sikh religion which was begun in India about 500 years ago by Guru Nanak

Soul The thinking, feeling part of a person, as opposed to their physical body. In many beliefs, the soul is said to live on after the person's physical body dies.

Synagogue A place where Jewish people worship.

Talmud A collection of Jewish writings dating from about 200 to 500 CE. It contains the thoughts of many early rabbis.

Tao A great power in the world taught by Lao-tzu, an ancient Chinese philosopher. The word Tao means 'the Way'.

Tirthankaras The twenty four great heroes or teachers of the Jain religion

Tirthas In Hindu belief, sacred crossing places between Heaven and Earth. The most sacred is Varanasi, a city on the banks of the holy River Ganges in India.

Torah The most sacred part of the Jewish scriptures. The five books of the Torah are written on scrolls and kept in the Holy Ark in the synagogue.

UFOs Unidentified Flying Objects, often thought to be alien spaceship.

Upanishad One of a group of ancient Hindu scriptures which talk about the relationship between people and Brahman (God)

Vaikuntha In Hindu belief, the Heaven of the god Vishnu

Valhalla In Viking legend, a magnificent hall in the land of the gods to which the souls of dead warriors were taken

Vishnu One of three main Hindu gods. The protector of the world.

Yad A special pointer used to point to the Torah scrolls because they are too precious to touch with the fingers

Yahrzeit A Jewish ceremony held on the anniversary of a person's death. A special candle is lit and the Kaddish prayer is said.

Zen A type of Buddhism followed in Japan and China. Zen Buddhists use meditation as the way to reach enlightenment.

Zodiac A band of the sky divided into twelve parts called the signs of the zodiac. These are used in astrology.

Zoroaster A holy man who lived in Persia (modern Iran) some 3,000 years ago

Zoroastrianism The ancient religion begun by Zoroaster. Its followers are called Zoroastrians or Parsis, meaning Persian.

INDEX

BIBLIOGRAPHY

Afterlife – the Complete Guide to Life After Death,
Carol Neiman & Emily Goldman, Boxtree, 1994

A History of Heaven: The Singing Silence, Jeffrey
Burton Russell, Princeton University Press,
1997

Angels, James Underhill, Element Books, 1995

Angels: An Endangered Species, Malcolm Godwin, Boxtree,
1993

Angels to Watch Over Me, Joanne Crosse, Element
Children's Books, 1998

Animal Spirits (Livingstone Wisdom series), Nicholas J.
Saunders, Macmillan, 1995

Heaven: A History, McDannel & Lang, Yale, 1988

Heaven – an illustrated history of the higher realms,
Timothy Freke, Godsfield Press, 1996

Hell – an illustrated history of the netherworld, Richard
Craze, Godsfield Press, 1996

History of Hell, A. Turner, Hale, 1995

Life After Death, Farnaz, Ma'sumian, Oneworld, 1995

Life After Death and the World Beyond, Jenny Randles &
Peter Hough, Piatkus, 1996

Religion, (Eyewitness Guides), Dorling Kindersley, 1996

Sacred Architecture, A. T. Mann, Element Books, 1993

The Atlas of Holy Places and Sacred Sites, Colin Wilson,
Dorling Kindersley, 1996

The Atlas of Sacred Places, James Harpur, BCA, 1994

*The Element Illustrated Encyclopedia of Animals in Nature,
Myth and Spirit*, Fran Pickering, Element Children's
Books, 1999

*The Element illustrated Encyclopedia of Mind, Body, Spirit
& Earth*, Joanna Crosse, Element Children's Books,
1998

The Elements of Astrology, Janis Huntley, Element
Books, 1990

The Elements of Native American Traditions, Arthur
Versluis, Element Books, 1993

The Elements of the Aborigine Tradition, James G. Cowan,
Element Books, 1992

The Elements of Reincarnation, A.T. Mann, Element
Books, 1995

The Elements of Shamanism, Nevill Drury, Element
Books, 1989

The Encyclopedia of Afterlife Beliefs and Phenomena, James
R. Lewis, Visible Ink, 1995

The Illustrated Book of Myths, Neil Philip, Dorling
Kindersley, 1995

The Illustrated Encyclopedia of World Religions, Ed. Chris
Richards, Element Books, 1997

The Little Book of Angel Wisdom, Peter Lamborn Wilson,
Element Books, 1997

The New Larousse Encyclopedia of Mythology, Crescent
Books, 1989

The Oxford Dictionary of World Religions, edited by John
Bowker, Oxford University Press, 1997

The Sacred Earth (Living Wisdom series), Brian Leigh
Molyneaux, Macmillan, 1995

The Tibetan Book of the Dead, edited by W. Y. Evans-
Wentz, Oxford University Press, 1984

The Travellers' Guide to Hell, Michael Pauls and Dana
Facaros, Cadogan, 1998

What's the Big Idea? Religion, Anita Ganeri, Hodder
Children's Books, 1998

World Mythology, the illustrated guide, edited by Roy
Willis, Simon and Schuster, 1993

Visions of Heaven and Hell, Richard Cavendish, Orbis,
1997

World Religions, John Bowker, Dorling Kindersley,
1997

ACKNOWLEDGEMENTS

From Anita Ganeri:

I would like to thank everyone who has helped make this book possible, providing me with heavenly quotes, inspiration and ideas. In particular, heartfelt thanks go to Nicky Barber and Catherine Chambers for their help with the monumental amounts of research and for their moral support. Special thanks also go to Merryl Hammond and Tami Hammond-Collins for their kindness in providing me with invaluable information about their own Baha'i faith. For their help with quotes, poems and photographs, I am hugely grateful to the following: Anne Clarke of the Jewish Resource Centre; Rasamandala Das of ISKON Educational services; Dr Puran Ganeri; Father Martin Robindra Ganeri O.P.; Anna Johnson and the children of Tyersal First School, Bradford; Rabbi Dr Michael Shire of the Centre for Jewish Education; Eden Silver-Myer; Carolyn Simon; Nicola, Thomas and Caitlin Wynne. And finally if there is a heaven, I hope that Roamer and Wallace are happy there.

ILLUSTRATION ACKNOWLEDGEMENTS

Grateful thanks to all the illustrators who have contributed such beautiful artwork for this title.

ABIGAIL CONWAY pp 15, 23, 40-41, 50-51, 56-57, 67, 97, 109, 112-113, 130, 138
ROSALIND HUDSON pp 39, 49, 78-79, 89, 136-137
NADINE FAYE JAMES pp 54-55, 75, 100, 110,
KATTY MCMURRAY pp 28-29, 36-37, 91, 126-127,
JILL NEWTON pp 9, 24-25, 27, 32-33, 42-43, 53, 60-61, 86-87, 102-103, 119, 128-129,
ROSEMARY WOODS pp 12-13, 17, 35, 45. 65, 68-69, 77, 83, 98-99, 116-117, 142-143

PHOTOGRAPH ACKNOWLEDGEMENTS

8 Musée du Petit Palais, Avignon /A. Guerrand
9 Victoria & Albert Museum Picture Library
14 ICOREC /Circa Photo Library
16 ET Archive /British Museum
18 Still Pictures /Hartmut Schwarzbach
19 The Bridgeman Art Library /Victoria & Albert Museum
20 Panos Pictures /Jean-Leo Dugast
21 (left) Panos Pictures /Ron Giling
21 (right) Victoria & Albert Museum Picture Library
22 ET Archive /British Library
26 Hutchison Library /Jon Burbank
28 (left) Image Select /Chris Fairclough
28 (right) Rex Features
32 ET Archive /Stadtmuseum, Trier, Germany
34 The Bridgeman Art Library /Oriental Museum, Durham University
41 ET Archive /Garrick Club, London
42 ICOREC /Circa Photo Library /Bipinchandra Mistry
44 Tony Stone Images /David Hiser
48 Werner Forman Archive /E. Strouhal
52 © The British Museum
53 The Bridgeman Art Library /Haynes Fine Art at The Bindery Galleries, Broadway
57 (top) Still Pictures /Gil Moti
57 (bottom) Werner Forman Archive /Philip Goldman Collection
62 Tony Stone Images /Ken Graham
63 ET Archive /Prado Museum
64 The Bridgeman Art Library /British Museum)
66 Tony Stone Images /Ken Graham
69 Popperfoto
70 Tony Stone Images /Nabeel Turner
71 ICOREC /Circa Photo Library /William Holtby
72 London Aerial Photo Library
73 Andes Press Agency /Carlos Reyes-Manzo
74 Still Pictures /Paul Harrison
76 The Hutchison Library /Michael Macintyre
82 Still Pictures /Mark Edwards
84 ET Archive /British Museum
85 The Bridgeman Art Library /British Museum
88 Fortean Picture Library /Paul Broadhurst
90 Werner Forman Archive /Private collection
92 Still Pictures /Thomas D. Mangelsen
93 Derby Museum & Art Gallery
96 The Dean and Chapter of Wells
98 Popperfoto
100-101 Tony Stone Images /Dale DeGabriele
106 (top) Andes Press Agency /Carlos Reyes-Manzo
106 (bottom)Andes Press Agency /Carlos Reyes-Manzo
107 Popperfoto
108 The Bridgeman Art Library /Rafael Valls Gallery

111 Tony Stone Images /Hilarie Kavanagh
120 The Bridgeman Art Library /Southampton City Art Gallery
121 (bottom) Werner Forman Archive /Schindler Collection, New York
121 (top) The Bridgeman Art Library /Oriental Museum, Durham University
122 Tony Stone Images /Hilarie Kavanagh
123 (top) ET Archive
123 (bottom) Tony Stone Images /Jean-Marc Trucet
131 Tibet Images /Ian Cumming
135 ET Archive /National Gallery, Oslo
141 Still Pictures /Regis Cavignaux
144 Still Pictures /Nigel Dickinson
145 Hulton Getty

TEXT ACKNOWLEDGEMENTS

W.H.AUDEN: 'Twelve Songs IX' from Collected Poems, edited by Edward Mendelson (Faber & Faber, 1991). Reprinted by permission of the publisher.

E.E.CUMMINGS: 'hist whist' from Complete Poems 1904–1962, edited by George J. Firmage (Norton, 1994),© 1991 by the Trustees for the E. E. Cummings Trust and George James Firmage. reprinted by permission of W.W. Norton & Company.

WALTER DE LA MARE: 'Me' from The Complete poems of Walter De La Mare (1969). Reprinted by permission of The Literary Trustees of Walter de la Mare, and the Society of Authors as their representative.

ANNE FRANK: From The Diary of a Young Girl: The Definitive Edition, edited by Otto H. Frank and Mirjam Pressler, translated by Susan Massotty (Viking, 1997), © The Anne Frank-Fonds, Basle, Switzerland, 1991; English translation © Doubleday, a division of Bantam Doubleday Dell Publishing Group Inc., 1995. Reprinted by permission of Penguin Books Ltd.

ANDREW LINZEY: from Animal Rites: Liturgies of Animal Care (SCM Press, 1999). Reprinted by permission of the publisher.

SIEGFRIED SASSOON: 'Everyone Sang' from Collected Poems 1908 – 1956 (Faber & Faber, 1984), copyright 1947, 1961 by Siegfried Sasoon. reprinted by permission of George Sassoon and Viking Penguin, a division of Penguin Putnam inc.

W. B. YEATS: 'He Wishes for the Cloths of Heaven' from Collected Poems (Picador, 1990). Reprinted by permission of A. P. Watt Ltd on behalf of Michael B. Yeats.

Every effort has been made to trace or contact all copyright holders. The publishers would be pleased to rectify any omissions brought to their notice at the earliest opportunity.